Additional Praise for
Live Gay, Retire Rich!

"Now that marriage equality is a reality, we have a lot of brushing up to do. Estate planning, tax laws, medical benefits, housing rights, healthcare and on and on. They have granted us the right to marry. The responsibility of understanding the law is ours. Here's your guide."

> — Harvey Fierstein
> Tony Award Winning Actor & Playwright

"*Live Gay, Retire Rich!* is a must-read book for same-sex couples who want financial security for themselves and their heirs. James Lange applies his legal and tax experience with common sense, sound calculations, and action steps in an "easy-to-read format.""

> — Ron Kelemen, CFP®
> The H Group, Inc., Salem, OR
> Author, *The Confident Retirement Journey —*
> *Your Personal & Financial Roadmap*

"Best-selling author, James Lange, has a richly deserved reputation for providing well-considered, practical advice on investing, retirement planning and tax management. Now he has turned his attention to the tremendous opportunities that have become available since the Supreme Court struck down a key provision of the Defense of Marriage Act. Same-sex couples will do themselves a huge favor by reading this book and acting on its advice."

> — Burton G. Malkiel
> Author, *A Random Walk Down Wall Street* (11th Edition)

*"**Live Gay, Retire Rich!** is a must read for LGBT couples wondering what is the best path for them pursue in regard to marriage. For many of my friends and family who are wrestling with this important issue, they often care more about fairness and access to marriage as an institution. Jim brings to the community a clear roadmap for how they can rationally approach the critical responsibilities and opportunities that might be afforded to them financially. I applaud his effort to use his legal and accounting expertise to help the community in such a practical manner."*

> — Tim McCarthy
> Author, *The Safe Investor: How to Make Your Money Grow in a Volatile Economy*

"It's about time! CPA and attorney Jim Lange has written the essential financial guide for same-sex couples. Brimming with examples, case studies, and easily understood graphs, Lange has laid out a path that is simple to understand, simple to follow, and extremely valuable. If you're part of the LGBT community, you need this book!"

> — Jan Cullinane
> Author, *The Single Woman's Guide to Retirement*

*"**Live Gay, Retire Rich!** makes it easy to learn the answers to all your questions about this topic, including many you might not have thought to ask."*

> — Kaye A. Thomas
> Author, *Go Roth!*

*"**Live Gay, Retire Rich!** is a must read, providing practical guidance on important planning issues. Financial planning for same-sex couples is evolving in response to changing federal and state laws, and Jim Lange's book provides invaluable advice in an easy to digest manner."*

> — Daniel S. Kern
> President and CIO, Advisor Partners

*"**Live Gay, Retire Rich!** shows you great ideas to help you achieve the most important financial goal of your life. Make your money last and go further than you ever thought possible."*

> — Brian Tracy, Speaker, Sales Trainer
> Author, *Getting Rich Your Own Way*

"Like a breath of fresh air, the doors are being kicked open that address what society is demanding—and that is same-sex couples are entitled to have their concerns and issues dealt with openly, consciously and appropriately. Kudos to Jim, for writing this terrific resource for planners, same-sex couples and other professionals who will benefit greatly from the knowledge, information and clarity provided. As a Financial Life Planner, these issues are essential to good practice and knowledge to help clients lead the life that is most important to them. This book is a terrific resource and each topic is clearly explained with concise and easy to understand examples provided. Great job!"

> — Michael F. Kay, CFP®
> President, Financial Life Focus, LLC

"*Live Gay, Retire Rich!* provides a wealth of valuable information. It covers retirement plans, Social Security, income taxes, trusts and estate and inheritance tax issues. Given the recent Supreme Court decision and changes in the tax code, this book is a must read for same-sex couples."

> — Mel Lindauer, Columnist, Forbes.com
> Co-Author, *The Bogleheads' Guide to Investing*
> Co-Author, *The Bogleheads' Guide to Retirement Planning*

"The IRS, Social Security and many other government agencies have rules that are different for straight and gay couples. Jim Lange, a retirement expert, has written *Live Gay, Retire Rich!* to increase their wealth, cut their taxes, and dramatically increase their financial security. This is a book I can highly recommend for the gay community and those who work to serve them. All proceeds will go to the civil rights organization, Freedom to Marry."

> — Taylor Larimore
> Co-Author, *The Bogleheads' Guide to Investing*
> Co-Author, *The Bogleheads' Guide to Retirement Planning*

"Jim provides some invaluable strategies for many loving couples who are currently deprived of the same rights as their fellow citizens. His suggestions could mean thousands of dollars to couples who happen to live in certain states. Change is the only changeless norm when it comes to retirement planning."

> — Dan Keppel
> Author, *Maximize Your Social Security Benefits and Retirement Income*

"After reading *Live Gay, Retire Rich!* and as the landscape changed radically in the past year, I realize we've made a great financial decision as well. Because my husband is back in school to change his career, we get a marriage bonus in our taxes. But even when we start paying the tax penalty as his income resumes, I calculate we'll still come out on top in the long run. So OK, you still have to first take love into consideration. But if finance is also playing into your decision, Lange's book should be at the top of your reading list."

— Yalman Onaran, *Bloomberg News*

"Jim Lange's book fills a much needed void by providing sound financial advice to same-sex couples. Implementing his recommendations can reduce taxes and permit same-sex couples to retire with dignity."

— Dan Solin
Author of the *Smartest* series of books

"With the Supreme Court ruling in U.S. v. Windsor holding that Section 3 of the Defense of Marriage Act (DOMA) is unconstitutional, planning for same-sex couples has been radically changed. Jim Lange has written an invaluable guide for both practitioners and their clients as to how to plan in this new environment. This book is an outstanding edition for the reader. The changing world of health insurance and Social Security benefits is thoroughly discussed in the book."

— Sid Kess, CPA, J.D., LL.M.
Author of hundreds of tax, financial and estate books
Voted *Most Influential Practitioner* by *CPA Magazine*

"In *Live Gay, Retire Rich!*, attorney and IRA expert Jim Lange explains how marriage can enhance the value of IRAs and Social Security, and how same-sex couples can now take advantage of these benefits."

— **Bruce Steiner, Attorney**
Kleinberg, Kaplan, Wolff & Cohen, P.C.

"There are so many laws both federal and state and they affect same-sex couples differently. As a CPA and an attorney, James Lange has more than 30 years in estate and retirement-planning experience. He has made a specialty of retirement planning for same-sex couples."

— Dan Poynter
Author, Publisher and Speaker

"Jim did a great job (again!) at reducing complex planning concepts to understandable action steps. The planning landscape for same-sex couples has and continues to change radically. You need accurate and current guidance. Harnessing the power of compounding investment earnings, and Jim's sage advice, will give you the best odds of a secure financial future."

— Martin M. Shenkman, CPA, MBA, JD
Author of 36 books and 700+ articles

"Recent changes in state and federal laws mean that same-sex couples can now claim many of the spousal benefits associated with IRAs, 401(k)s, estate taxes, Social Security, and government-subsidized health insurance. *Live Gay, Retire Rich!* helps you navigate the bewildering maze of rules and regulations, and avoid tax-planning mistakes that could sabotage your retirement plans. Jim Lange explains how you and your partner can manage two incomes, save on health insurance, maximize Social Security benefits for both of you, and transfer your wealth to your heirs. It is never too early (or too late!) to start planning."

— Martha Maeda, Author
Retire Rich With Your Roth IRA, Roth 401k and Roth 403b:
Investment Strategies for Your Roth IRA Explained Simply

"An eye-opening book! Read it now and secure your future. Delay and you'll pay later. I urge you to read this book right now."

— Dr. Joe Vitale
Author, *Attract Money Now*

"Jim Lange has taken the question-marks out of planning for same-sex couples. I highly recommend you not only read, but use this book!"

— Deena B Katz, CFP®
Associate Professor, Texas Tech University
Department of Personal Financial Planning

"In *Live Gay, Retire Rich!*, Lange not only jigsaws the pieces together for the LGBT community, but also provides great advice for the straight community. By using well thought out examples and clear graphs, even the most finance-challenged among us can follow along and be better able to meet our retirement goals."

— Bart Astor
Author, *Roadmap for the Rest of Your Life*

"If you are part of a same-sex couple, get hold of this book! James Lange has provided crucially needed answers for anyone, especially same-sex partners. If you want to build retirement wealth, I highly recommend you obtain this much-needed book."

— Ted Nicholas
Advertising Consultant, Speaker

LIVE *Gay* RETIRE RICH!

Retire Secure for Same-Sex Couples

JAMES LANGE
CPA/ATTORNEY

Lange Legal Group, LLC
2200 Murray Avenue
Pittsburgh, PA 15217
412.521.2732
admin@paytaxeslater.com

© Copyright 2015

Cartoons by Dave McCoy

ISBN-13: 9780990358855

Contents

Foreword

After decades of struggle, sacrifice, and storytelling, through persuasion and persistence, battles and building, our Freedom to Marry campaign has triumphed and we have won marriage nationwide. Couples throughout the land can now share in joy and meaning, as well as the rules, responsibilities and respect, that marriage brings. The marriage conversation, with all its power to continue changing hearts and minds, has now arrived in every corner of the country. We can now build on the momentum of our marriage win to advance the work that still remains to ensure that all people are fully free and equal no matter where they live.

Having the freedom to marry and the respect that lawful marriages are due happily presents gay couples with important financial opportunities, consequences, and decisions.

To help navigate this new landscape and think through the decisions now open to all, tax, retirement, and estate planning expert Jim Lange is stepping forward to add his voice. Jimmy (as I knew him in high school *um–um–um* years ago…) has written ***Live Gay, Retire Rich!*, *Retire Secure for Same-Sex Couples***, addressing the complexities of retirement planning amid all this momentum and change. It's the latest in a series of retirement-advice books Lange has authored, to great acclaim.

I am no tax expert, but it's clear to me that ***Live Gay, Retire Rich!*, *Retire Secure for Same-Sex Couples*** raises the right questions, gives lots of excellent advice, provides compelling examples, and backs up its claims with numerical analysis—*running the numbers*, as Jim calls it. ***Live Gay, Retire Rich!*** is a solid, helpful, mostly easy read on the application of tax, IRA, retirement, and death issues (for any married couple, actually) that offers an easy-to-understand analysis of the differences and benefits applicable to same-sex couples.

Because every couple's situation is different and some big questions may need in-depth discussion to resolve, the book may not (in fact cannot) produce ironclad solutions for all. But, it will challenge and help same-sex couples to think about what is right for them and point them in the right direction. While people may still need to consult their own tax and estate-planning advisers, and, in some cases, Freedom to Marry's legal partners such as Lambda Legal, Gay & Lesbian Advocates & Defenders (GLAD), National Center for Lesbian Rights (NCLR), and the ACLU, Jim's advice and recommendations are a good starting point for same-sex couples now finally free to share in marriage and all its protections and responsibilities.

Jim has generously pledged the proceeds from this book to Freedom to Marry, now in a smart, strategic wind-down and hand-off to our movement colleagues as we harness the marriage conversation to the work ahead—and naturally, I appreciate that. But what I really appreciate is his bringing his expertise to bear on helping the couples for whom we have won the freedom to marry. They, like all married couples, want to make strong, smart decisions and want and deserve to enjoy the security and opportunities that marriage as well as good financial planning brings.

Having just invested 32 year of my time and energy in winning the freedom to marry... I know the value of a good investment, and know how sweet it is to win! We all win when families are stronger and the law is fairer. And who—even an activist—doesn't want to retire secure?

— Evan Wolfson
Founder and President,
Freedom to Marry

Acknowledgments

Though my name is listed as author, the genuine truth is that this book is really a monumental team effort. I and the readers who find value in these pages are indebted to a team of the best CPAs, attorneys, financial planners, writers and other professionals that I could possibly hope to work with.

Shirl Trefelner, CPA, made major contributions to the "number crunching" effort which, in many ways is the backbone of the book, by preparing many of the graphs and charts contained in the chapters. She also proved amazingly sensitive in making sure the language in the book appropriately fitted her graphs and charts. She was particularly generous with her time, and she didn't complain (ok, maybe a little) about doing the work despite a heavy tax season workload. She has become the principle "number cruncher" for our LGBT clients.

Karen Mathias, Esq., is our resident Social Security expert and nit-picked us to death to get the Social Security chapter perfectly legally accurate. I kept trying to keep it simple. She wanted it technically perfect. Ultimately, we compromised; the Social Security chapter, somewhat, though not completely, satisfied my desire for simplicity, and somewhat, though not completely, satisfied her desire for being technically correct. Karen is also one of two estate attorneys who drafts wills and trusts for our LGBT clients.

Carol Palmer is another one of my employees who made substantial contributions. Carol really cares about getting everything exactly right. Fairly often I was happy with the way a particular thought was expressed, but Carol wanted to make sure virtually every detail was explained. For you engineers and quantitative types that like proof of the concept offered, you can thank Carol for being so thoughtful and detailed. You can also thank her for ignoring me when I spoke about deadlines and she just methodically did what she thought had to be done to prove the appropriate statement.

Steven T. Kohman, Certified Public Accountant, Certified Specialist in Retirement Planning, Certified Specialist in Estate Planning, has worked for me for over 18 years. Steve combines his extensive tax background with his superb quantitative and computer skills. Much of the quantitative analysis done in this book started with Steve's analysis that he did for our flagship book, *Retire Secure! A Guide to Getting the Most Out of What You've Got.*

Matt Schwartz, Esq., is an exceptionally bright and gifted IRA and estate attorney who has worked with me for 11 years. I am proud to have him as a colleague. He works closely with many of our LGBT clients to complete the documentation necessary to implement our recommended planning solutions. It is rare to find such a quantitatively gifted attorney.

Cynthia Nelson, our editor plus, has been working with me for over 15 years. During this period, she has had full editing and writing responsibilities for virtually all my published works. She is a rare find. She cuts through some of the technical and legal jargon that I sometimes fall into and expresses complex thoughts in a way the lay reader can understand. She also allows me to express my humanity, and she adds touches of her own that make reading the book a better experience.

Amanda Cassady-Schweinsberg and Eric Emerson, our marketing director and internet marketing director respectively made a monumental effort to get this book in your hands.

Thanks to Dave McCoy for your great cartoons. I had to look up his name because I think of him as Dave Toons.

To John Kremer, my "rock-star book consultant," thank you for your patience with a difficult client. You helped with a lot of behind the scenes stuff most people don't think about.

I want to thank some of the experts who have helped me with marketing, publicity and book sales, both Marie Swift and Al Martin of Impact Communications, Bob Bly, a great copywriter, and Tom Antion, an internet guru.

I want to give a special recognition to Evan Wolfson, founder of Freedom to Marry, who wrote the foreword. Evan is a modern day civil rights champion. He has supported my efforts from day one by appearing on my radio show and helping promote the book. All proceeds of the book will go to Evan's organization, Freedom to Marry and to the successor organization.

I also want to thank all the pre-release readers and reviewers of *Live Gay, Retire Rich!*. Special thanks go to Billie Jean King, Martin Sheen, Ed Slott, CPA and Jane Bryant Quinn and so many others who provided glowing testimonials. Your support means more to me than I can adequately express.

I must also convey my gratitude to my other full-time employees who provide so much help in my practice that without them, the book could never have been written: They have also been around for a long time giving both to me personally and to our company great stability: Glenn Venturino, CPA (how can I properly thank you for 27 years of superb service to our clients); Sandy Proto, thank you for 22 years of superb service as office manager (without Sandy the office would cease to function); Alice Davis, 12 years, who is so wonderful and personable with our clients and is the first to jump on board when anything needs to be done; Donna Master, 17 years, who keeps our books, which would certainly be a shambles without her dedicated precision; and Daryl Ross, 16 years, our legal administrative assistant/master tax return compiler who rolls up her sleeves and gets it done year after year.

Thanks also to other staff members who make life livable: Curt Borowsi, Diane Markel, CPA (14 years) and Tanya Chiu.

Special thanks also go to our joint venture partners who provide the investment arm of the assets-under-management side of our business. Thanks to P.J. DiNuzzo and his team at DiNuzzo Index Advisors, Inc. and Charlie Smith and his team at Fort Pitt Capital Group, Inc. We could not do what we do without both of your firms.

There is a special subcontractor who works on my behalf whom I want to thank. Stephen May, my webmaster for 18 years! How can I properly thank you? Stephen did the web work for the first version of **www.outestateplanning. com** in 2002!

To matters of the heart, a special thanks to my wife, Cindy Lange. She is probably the only woman alive who could put up with being married to me. (If you think I am overly being solicitous, just ask my employees; they will confirm that being married to me would be extremely difficult, and few could put up with me). Her imprint is on every page of the book. Cindy has been enormously resourceful in many areas and has made both significant direct and indirect contributions to the book. This book would never have happened without her help, support, and love.

Finally, thank you to my 20-year-old daughter, Erica. Erica, is a computer science and engineering student, whom I love dearly. I wish everyone had her open attitude about people of different sexual orientations, race, background, etc.

Thank you all.

Introduction

Should You Marry for Money?

Ok, that is a tongue-in-cheek question—we all know that's a risky proposition. But, in point of fact, there are some very favorable tax, estate planning and social security maximization strategies that are only available to married couples and not available to couples who are not married and just living together. Full disclosure: I offer *no advice* on the emotional pro and cons of marriage—I leave that to other experts. What I do offer, however, is a solid analysis of the financial implications of marrying versus remaining single.

So why should you read this book? Because the knowledge you stand to gain from reading it can make the difference between spending your golden years doing the things you have always dreamed about, or living in poverty.

You may know that straight married couples have had access to multiple tax and estate planning and social security maximization strategies that can increase wealth, reduce taxes, and dramatically improve a family's financial security. And now, with the Supreme Court ruling, all those advantages are fully available to same-sex couples as well. But it also means that you may find yourself making the same financial mistakes that straight couples have been making for years—mistakes that could have disastrous consequences for you and your spouse/partner. This book will address the advantages and disadvantages of marriage in terms of financial decisions that have to be made at all ages, but will likely have the greatest significance for couples aged 60 or older

Most committed same-sex couples, especially where at least one member is age 60 or older, should, either on their own or with an advisor, evaluate whether it makes *financial sense* to marry and if so, what proactive steps they can take to secure their financial future.

Let's look at an example.

There were two identically situated same-sex couples[1]: they had the same amount of money, invested identically, and spent identically too. There was

---

[1] These couples are fictional. But the outcomes are accurate based upon certain reasonable assumptions covered in detail in Chapter 8.

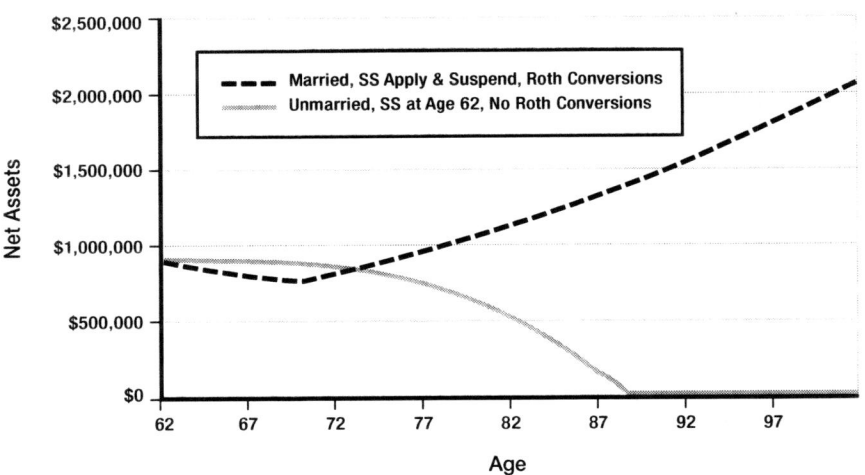

Unmarried vs. Married
Net Assets Available for Retirement Years

only one big difference: the first couple *did not* read ***Live Gay, Retire Rich!*** and plan for their future using our advice, but the second couple did.

The graph above illustrates the difference in their future finances using reasonable assumptions. Using the proactive strategies recommended in this book, one same-sex couple (the dashed line) enjoys a comfortable retirement, and still has $1,427,275 at age 90. The other couple, who didn't take our advice, runs out of money at age 90. Which couple are you going to be?

This graph, as well as a breakdown of the decisions that each couple made in order to achieve the results shown, are covered in greater detail later in this book. The point I wanted to make to you, though, is that committed same-sex couples now have an opportunity to increase their wealth, maximize social security, cut their taxes, and dramatically increase their financial security.

This book will show you that the difference between making good decisions and bad decisions over the term of your life can be startling. For example, the advantage gained for couples with a combined net worth of more than $1,000,000 simply by marrying can be often measured in terms of hundreds of thousands of dollars (sometimes well over $1,000,000 as seen above). For couples with a net worth of less than $1,000,000, the difference will not be as great, but good planning could mean the difference between a comfortable retirement and, when one spouse dies, the surviving spouse/partner being financially secure and living comfortably versus living out his or her remaining

years in poverty. (Death is never an easy topic, but when you work in estate planning facing reality is critically important.)

I want to make sure that, no matter what happens to the stock market, and no matter what happens to their partners or spouses—my clients and readers will always have food on the table, shelter over their heads, gas in the car, and a little bit of money for Saturday night. I also cover some of the potential disadvantages of getting married. Sometimes getting married can increase the cost of your health care coverage. In addition, in some situations you may be taking on the long-term-care costs of your partner by getting married.

I wrote this book because I believe that it is critical to get the facts out to everyone in the LGBT community. Committed same-sex couples have spent much of their lives being treated financially as though they were "single" people —especially in the eyes of the government. The information in this book is not intended to be a prescription for every couple; rather, it is meant to open your eyes to possibilities, both positive and negative, that same-sex couples did not need to consider before same-sex marriage was even a possibility. Given that caveat, however, I believe that the strategies that I present in this book will provide enormous benefits for most same-sex couples. And if you are armed with common sense information, I believe you will be in a much better position to come out ahead if you are considering making a life changing decision.

Let me be frank about my agenda. If I can influence thousands and preferably hundreds of thousands of same-sex couples to make the best possible financial decisions, it would be a great thing. I want you to keep as much money as possible in your family's pocket—you, your spouse/partner and (if you have any) your children and grandchildren or nieces, nephews, and other family members—so you and your family can lead the best life possible.

My second agenda is to potentially attract a limited number of same-sex couples who may choose to work with me and my business after reading this book.

I know that many individuals do not have the time or patience to read through all the details in a financial book. If all you want to know is the "answer," and, at least for now, don't care how I arrived at my recommendations, then please enjoy the charts in the next section, "The Essence of the Book Boiled Down to Nine Graphs." If you want to learn more, continue reading, it might make you marry for money!

Also, I would like to keep the dialogue alive. Please contact me with feedback or any questions you might have. Contact information and additional resources are included at the back of the book.

— Jim Lange

1

||||||||||||||||||||||||||

The Essence of the Book Boiled Down to 9 Graphs

Live Gay, Retire Rich! quantitatively compares various courses of action for same-sex couples. For those who don't want to read through the explanation and detail, just looking at the following nine graphs could provide critical information with a minimum of reading effort. Please be aware that the recommendations beneath each figure will be advantageous in most situations, but not for everyone.

— Jim Lange

1

Taking Advantage of Retirement Plans Rather than
Savings Outside Retirement Plans

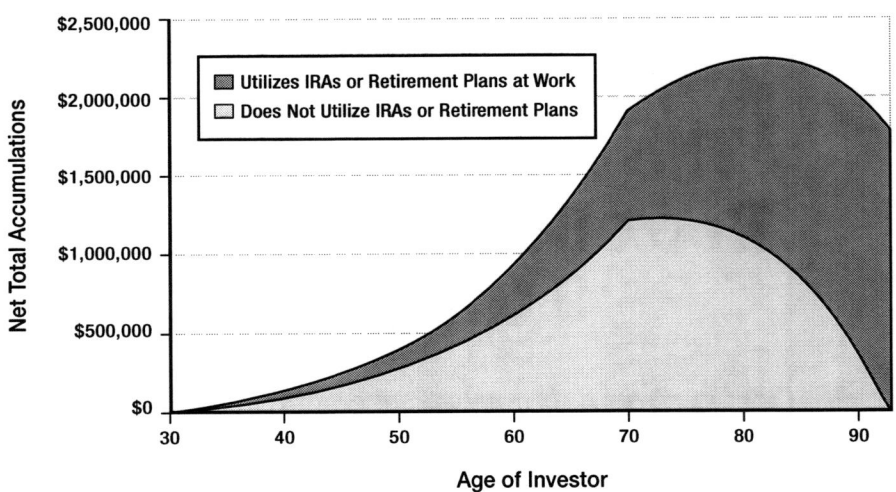

It's better to save in IRAs and retirement plans versus saving in after-tax accounts (regular investments outside IRAs or retirement plans).

This graph shows the total net assets* for two identically situated people, except one contributes to his retirement plan at work and the other saves outside the retirement plan. They each have the same earnings, invest the same out of pocket amount at the same rate, have the same tax bracket, spend the same, etc. The difference is dramatic.

The lesson: Don't pay taxes now, pay taxes later—during the accumulation stage while you are working.

Please see page 14.

*We measure $100 in an IRA as $75 net assets because there is a $25 income tax associated with the $100 IRA. This applies to this and the following graph.

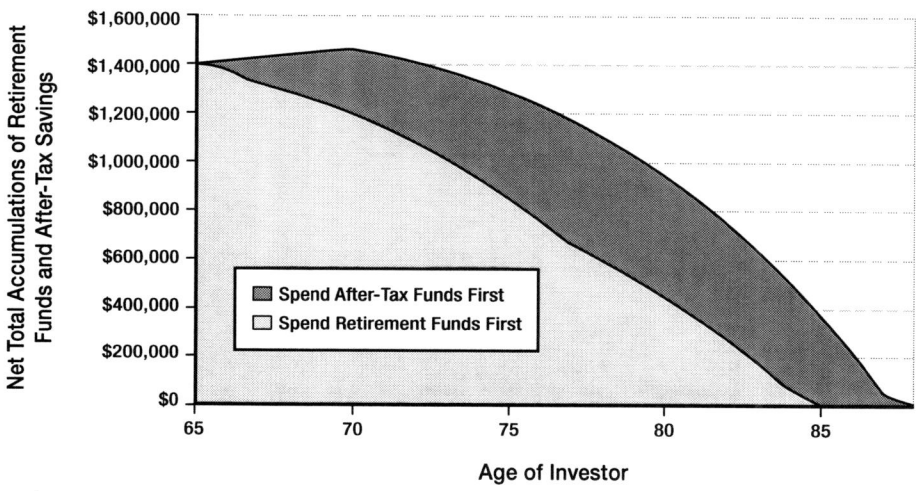

It's generally best to spend assets in this order: 1) after-tax savings
2) traditional IRA and retirement assets.

Of course, at age 70 you will have to take money out of your IRA. Given a choice, however, you should spend your after-tax savings first. You will have more money if you keep your money growing tax-deferred for as long as possible.

Don't pay taxes now, pay taxes later—when you are retired and in the distribution stage.

Please see page 15.

**Inheriting an IRA from a
Spouse vs. an Unmarried Partner**

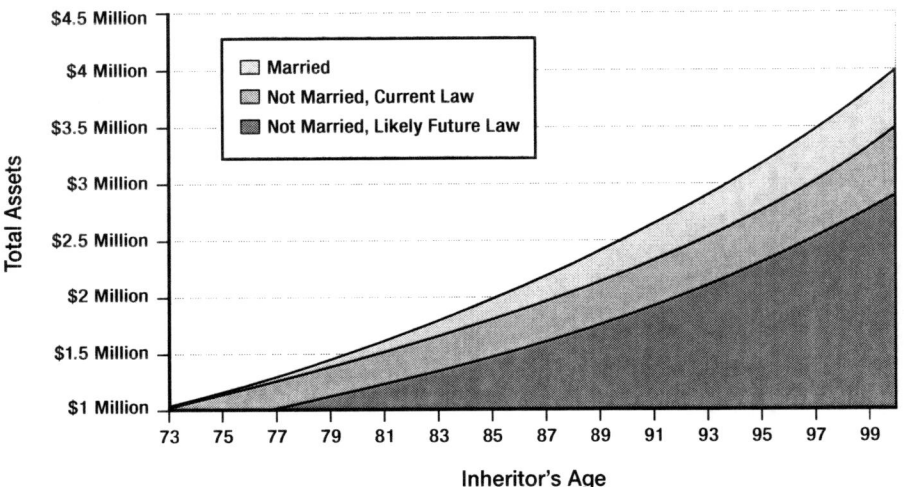

Inheritor's Age

***Estate Planning: Get married to provide maximum IRA and retirement plan
assets for your partner after your death.***

This graph shows the total assets for two individuals who each inherit a
$1,000,000 IRA at the age of 72—one inherits from his spouse and the other
from his unmarried partner. The tax laws will allow a surviving spouse to keep
the money growing tax-deferred much longer than they allow for a surviving
partner. Under the projected law changes for *Inherited IRAs*, the scenario is
even worse for the unmarried survivor. Getting married allows your surviving
spouse to pay taxes later than if you stayed unmarried.

Don't pay taxes now, pay taxes later—even after you die.

Please see page 37.

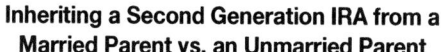

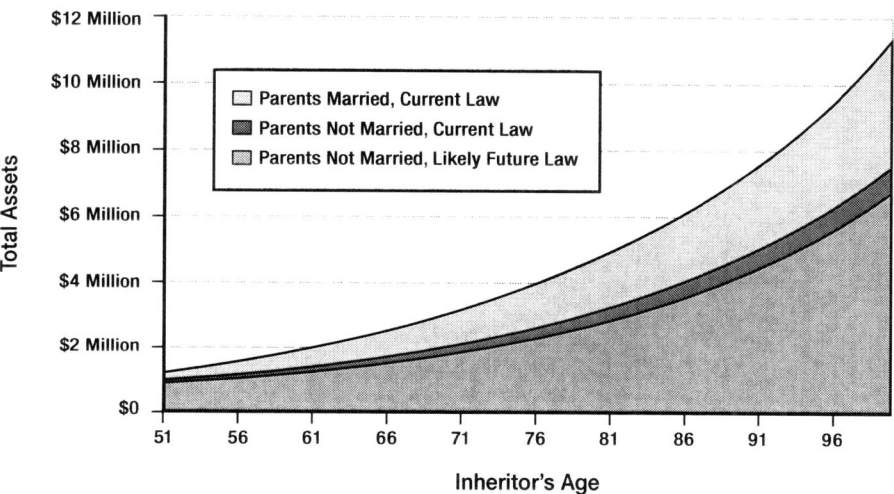

Inheriting a Second Generation IRA from a
Married Parent vs. an Unmarried Parent

Inheritor's Age

Estate Planning: Get married to provide maximum assets for your children or other heirs after both you and your partner die.

This graph shows the difference to the eventual heir depending on whether the person leaving him the IRA had married vs. had not gotten married. Tax laws favor the married couple when one of the spouses dies, allowing the surviving spouse to "pay taxes later." In addition to this advantage, tax laws favor heirs of a married couple. When the surviving spouse dies, his heir is permitted to "stretch" the IRA and "pay taxes (much) later."

Tax laws penalize the unmarried couple. The first time an IRA is inherited by a non-spouse, the unmarried partner is forced to "pay taxes sooner." The rules are even less favorable for the surviving partner's heir, forcing him to "pay taxes (much) sooner."

Don't pay taxes now, pay taxes later—even after both you and your partner/ spouse are gone.

Please see page 38.

Starting Social Security Benefits at 62 Years Old vs. 70 Years Old

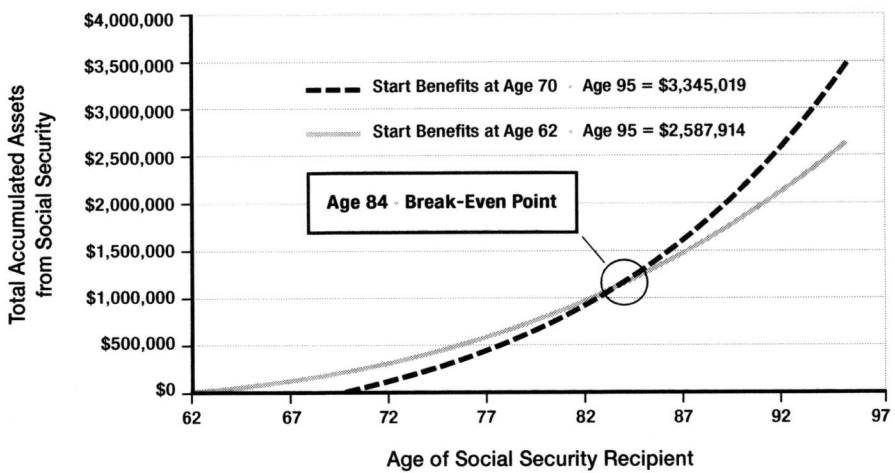

Age of Social Security Recipient

Independent of getting married, it's better to wait until 70 to take Social Security than electing to take Social Security at 62.

The graph shows the total of all Social Security benefits received, plus interest, by two different people with identical earnings records. One begins collecting Social Security at age 62 and the other begins collecting at age 70.

Your benefit will be 76% plus the cost of living adjustment larger if you wait until age 70 to start collecting Social Security, as compared to starting at 62.

The longer you live, the more you may need that larger benefit.

Please see page 49.

Unmarried vs. Married Using Apply & Suspend for Social Security

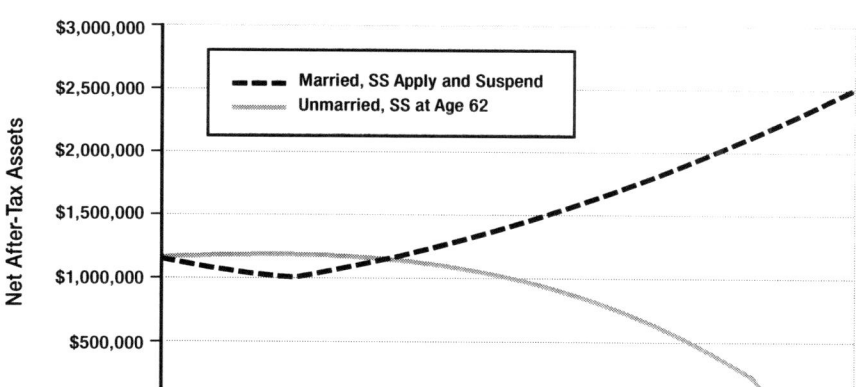

It's better to Apply and Suspend Social Security benefits until age 70.

The graph compares the net total assets for a married couple who uses a technique we often recommend called *Apply and Suspend*, to the assets of an unmarried couple who cannot take advantage of that strategy. Both couples start out with the same amount of money, spend the same amount of money and have identical earnings records. In this scenario, none of the individuals die. The unmarried couple runs out of money at age 92, while the married couple's assets are over $2,000,000 and growing.

Please see page 58.

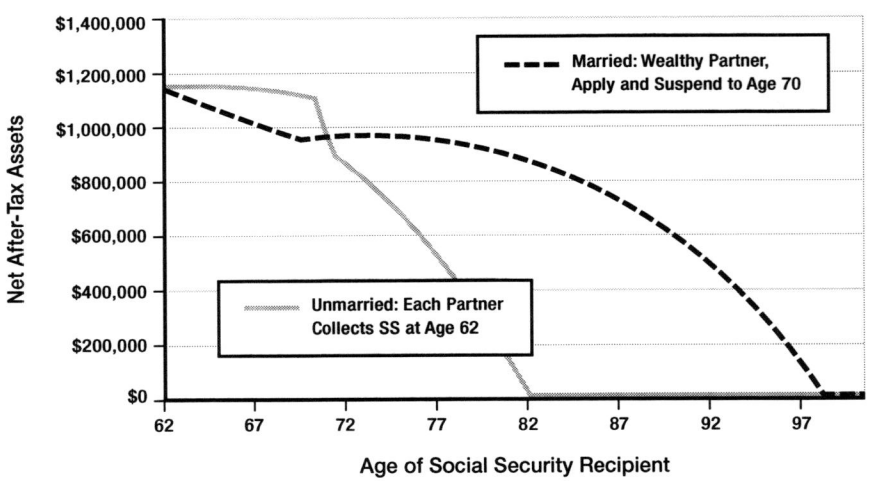

Unmarried vs. Married Using Social Security Apply & Suspend with an Early Death

Age of Social Security Recipient

Estate Planning: If the partner/spouse with the stronger earnings record dies first, it's much better for the surviving partner if they had been married and utilized the Apply and Suspend strategy.

This graph shows the total after-tax assets for two couples: one married, using the *Apply and Suspend* technique for Social Security benefits, and one unmarried, unable to use that strategy. Both couples start out with the same amount of money, spend the same amount of money and have identical earnings records.

At the age of 70, the higher wage earner of the two couples dies. The surviving partner/spouse lives off of their savings and their Social Security benefits. The money lasts longer in the married scenario, mainly because by using the *Apply and Suspend* technique, the partner with the stronger earnings record increased his benefit by waiting, and the survivor is able to collect a much higher Social Security benefit, known as a "spousal survivor benefit," based upon his spouse's wages.

Please note if the couple never gets married, they can't use the *Apply and Suspend* technique nor is there a survivor benefit.

Please see page 59.

Following vs. Ignoring the Advice in this Book:
Assets for Dependent Spouse/Partner After Death of Higher Wage Earner

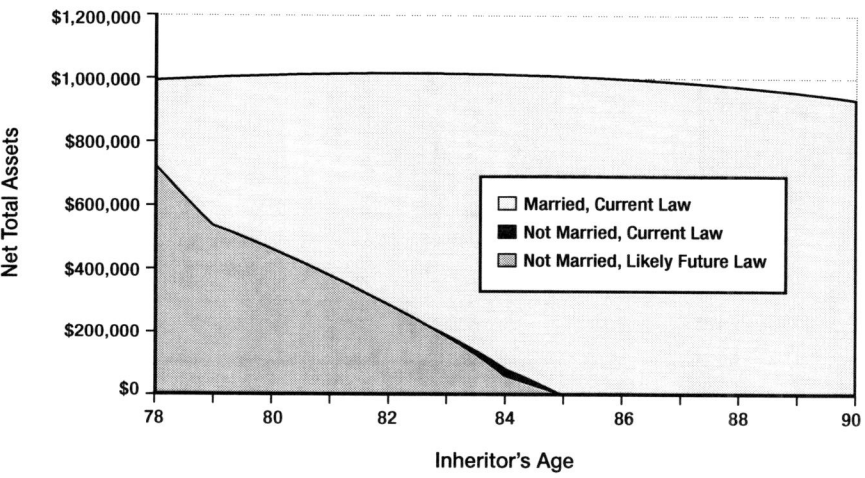

***Best case scenario for the surviving partner is if the couple gets married,
Applies and Suspends Social Security to age 70, makes Roth IRA conversions, and takes Spousal Social Security benefits at 66.***

The graph shows the total net assets for two people: one who followed all of the advice in this book and one who did not. In this scenario, the higher wage earner dies first at age 78. Because the married couple followed the advice in this book, the couple accumulated $300,000 in additional funds between the ages of 62 and 70, by taking advantage of *Apply and Suspend* for Social Security and by making Roth IRA Conversions.

After one spouse dies, the married survivor has further advantages over the unmarried survivor: he can collect higher social security benefits based on his spouse's wages and can leave money in the inherited IRAs and retirement plans growing tax deferred much longer.

Please see page 110.

Adult Child Inherits Assets from Widowed Parent

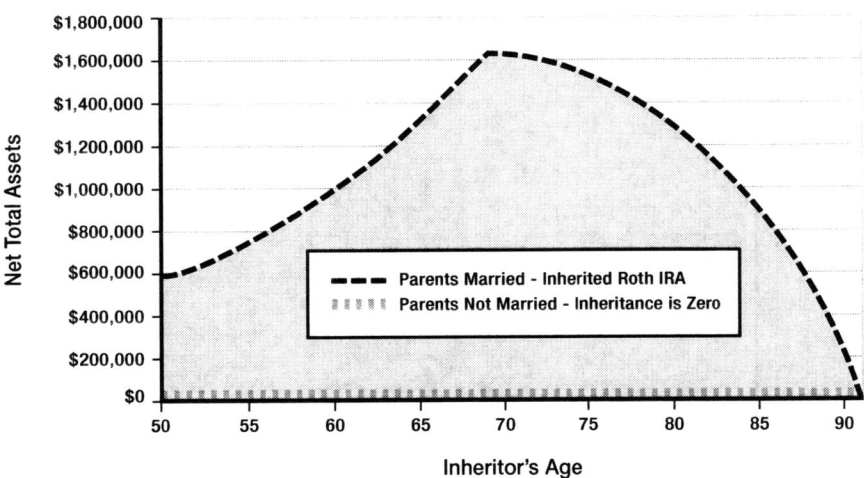

Inheritor's Age

The only scenario with money available for the next generation inheritance is if the parents married, used the Apply and Suspend strategy for Social Security, and optimized Roth IRA conversions.

In this example, if they didn't get married, took Social Security early, and didn't make any Roth IRA conversions, the adult child doesn't inherit anything.

Please see page 116.

2

||||||||||||||||||||||

Optimizing
IRAs & Retirement Plans
for Same-Sex Couples

*A man has made at least a start on discovering the meaning of
human life when he plants shade trees under which he knows
full well he will never sit.*

— Elton Trueblood (1900-1994)

Main Topics

- What is the difference between inheriting an IRA or retirement plan from my partner *vs.* my spouse?

- Why your marital status makes a difference in how much you, and even your heirs, are required to withdraw from an inherited IRA.

- Why beneficiaries should continue to withdraw the least possible amount (the required minimum distribution) from an inherited IRA.

> # KEY IDEA
>
> Committed same-sex couples should consider getting married to take advantage of the considerable financial benefits marriage confers with respect to inherited IRAs and retirement plans.

Overview of IRAs and Retirement Plans

The potentially life changing financial advantages that have only been available for married straight couples are now available for same-sex couples—but only if you get married and take the appropriate action. The difference between getting married and taking the appropriate action vs. not getting married could mean the difference between financial security for the surviving partner, and a life of financial struggle.

The following chapter is somewhat technical and is included for those who are willing to get immersed in the details. If you are not, here are the most important points:

- Being married is extremely advantageous for inheriting IRAs.

- While working, contribute to a retirement plan.

- While retired, subject to exception, spend your "after-tax" dollars first.

- Plan for your heirs, hopefully your spouse, to extend the time you have to pay taxes on your IRA or retirement plan after your death.

Background

The Power of Contributing to Retirement Plans While Working

In the first two editions of my book *Retire Secure! Pay Taxes Later* (Wiley, 2006 and 2009) I go to great lengths to prove that, in general, it makes sense to *"pay taxes later."* While you are working, you should contribute the maximum allowed to your retirement plan (or a combination of retirement plans). This is a method of paying taxes later because, with a traditional IRA, a 401(k), or other type of defined contribution plan, you and/or your employer make tax-deductible contributions to your plan and you don't pay the taxes on your contributions until you withdraw the money during your retirement. To see why this is important, please take a look at the graph below. It represents two individuals, Mr. Pay Taxes Later and Mr. Pay Taxes Now. They are identical in all respects except for one fundamental difference in their investment strategy:

- Both men begin saving at age 30.

- They contribute $8,000 to their accounts in the first year, and continue to do so until they are 70 years old. Their savings amounts are increased by 2.5% for inflation every year.

- Neither of the companies they work for match their contributions. (This is just to simplify the calculation. Adding in employer matching makes the argument even stronger.)

However,

- Mr. Pay Taxes Later has his entire $8,000 withheld from his paycheck and deposited to his tax-deferred 401(k). (The analysis would be identical if he contributed the money to a traditional deductible IRA, although $8,000 is well over the current allowed IRA contribution limit.)

- Mr. Pay Taxes Now chooses to not have any retirement funds withheld from his paycheck. He pays income taxes on his full wages, with the intention of saving for his retirement by investing the $8,000 he chose to not contribute to his tax-deferred retirement plan. He has to pay income tax immediately on the $8,000. After the 25% income tax is paid, he has only 75% of the $8,000, or $6,000, left to invest in his brokerage account.

Now, to be fair, Mr. Pay Taxes Later will have to pay taxes eventually. When he is retired, for every dollar he wants to withdraw he has to take out $1.33. He pockets the dollar and pays $0.33 in taxes (25 % of $1.33). If Mr. Pay Taxes Now withdraws a dollar, subject to some capital gains taxes, it's all his. At age 92, however, Mr. Pay Taxes Now has depleted his funds entirely, whereas Mr. Pay Taxes Later has $1,941,727 left in his retirement plan. Given reasonable assumptions and all things being equal, following the adage "Don't pay taxes now—pay taxes later" can be worth almost $2 million over your lifetime.

As you can see in Figure 2.1, over the long term, Mr. Pay Taxes Later ends up with significantly more money because he used his retirement plan at work. Assumptions for Figure 2.1 are shown in the footnote below[1].

Figure 2.1

Taking Advantage of Retirement Plans Rather than Savings Outside Retirement Plans

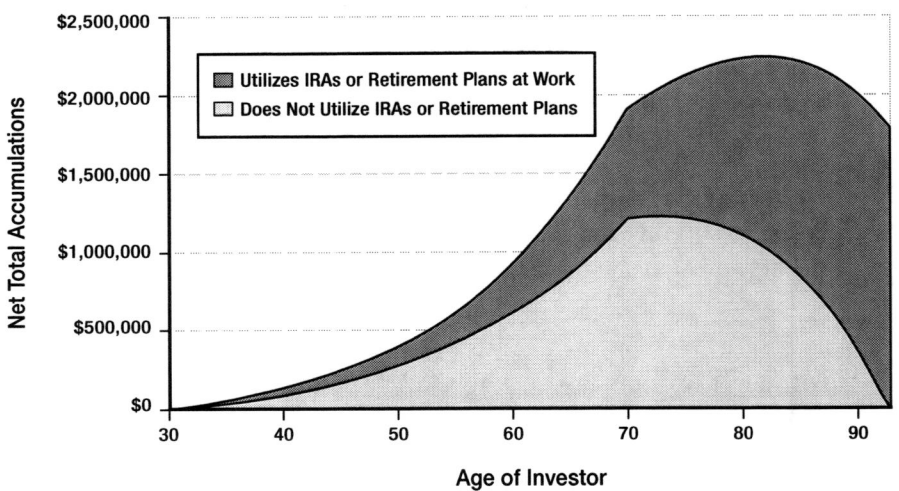

Age of Investor

Which Dollars Should You Spend First in Retirement?

Now, to continue the *"pay taxes later"* theme, let's look at which dollars you should spend first, after you retire.

When you retire, if you have money outside IRAs and retirement plans, I want you to spend your after-tax dollars *first*, before your IRA or retirement plan dollars. If you can afford it, I don't want you to take any distributions from your IRA or retirement plan until you have to—after age 70½ —when you must begin to take required minimum distributions (RMD). By taking only

---

[1] 1. We use a conservative investment rate of return of 6%, including 70% capital appreciation, with 15% portfolio turnover rate, 15% dividend income, and 15% interest income.

2. Starting at age 71, spending from both investors' accounts is equal to the required minimum distributions (RMDs) from Mr. Pay Taxes Later's retirement plan, less related income taxes.

3. Mr. Pay Taxes Later withdraws only the required minimum distribution (RMD), pays the 25% income tax due on his distribution, and spends the rest. Mr. Pay Taxes Now spends the same amount, plus he pays income taxes due on his interest, dividends and realized capital gains.

4. Ordinary tax rates are 25%. Capital gains tax rates are 15%. Dividends are taxed as capital gains.

the required minimum distributions, you keep more of your money growing tax-deferred. That is another form of paying taxes later. If you spend your IRA dollars, you have to pay taxes now.

Figure 2.2 below is similar to the previous graph except that it represents the distribution phase, not the accumulation phase. This graph shows the difference between two identically situated people with identical investments, tax rates, etc. except one chooses to spend their after-tax dollars first (pay taxes later) and the other chooses to spend his IRA or retirement plan first (pay taxes now).

Figure 2.2
Benefits of Spending After-Tax Savings Before IRAs
and Other Retirement Assets

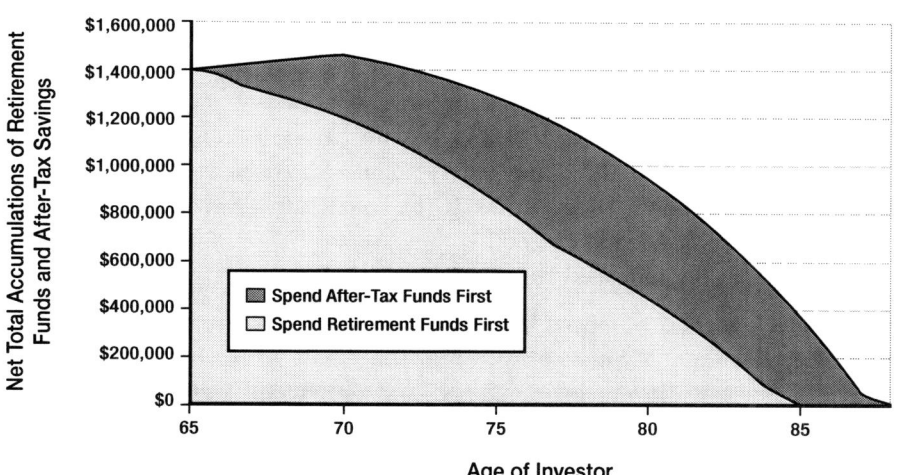

Depending on the time frame and which dollars you spend first, the quantifiable advantage of *"paying taxes later"* can be hundreds of thousands of dollars. Assumptions for Figure 2.2 are shown in the footnote below[2].

---

[2] 1. An investment rate of return of 6%

   2. Rate of inflation is 3%

   3. Starting at age 65, both investors spend $96,000 per year.

   4. Starting at age 65, both investors have beginning After Tax Funds of $300,000 and beginning retirement funds of $1,100,000.

   5. Both investors receive $30,000 per year in Social Security benefits adjusted annually for cost of living allowances, but have no other income.

The Impact of Marriage on the Accumulation Years

Marriage may afford you additional possibilities to contribute to retirement plans that may not be available to you as an unmarried individual; on the other hand, marriage might also eliminate possibilities to contribute.

One of the first rules for contributing to an IRA, including a Roth IRA is that you must have earned income. If you are *not* married, and your partner is not working, he or she will not be allowed to contribute to a Traditional or Roth IRA. But the rules are different for married couples. If you marry, your spouse will be able to contribute to an IRA or Roth IRA (or you will be able to contribute on his or her behalf, based on your own income). In this case, marriage makes it possible for you to save more money in the tax-deferred or tax-free environment.

For example, consider the couple Anne and Susan. Anne earns $150,000 per year and is not covered by a retirement plan where she works. Susan does not work outside the home. If they are unmarried, Anne can contribute to a traditional IRA for herself, but Susan has no earned income and so cannot contribute to an IRA at all. If they marry, then both Anne and Susan can each contribute to their own IRAs. In 2015, the maximum they can each contribute to their IRAs is $5,500 ($6,500 if they are age 50 or older), although this amount is generally indexed every year for inflation.

Here is a second potential benefit to marriage. Taxpayers whose incomes exceed certain limits are not permitted to contribute to Roth IRAs, and those income limits are different for married and unmarried individuals (refer to table below). If your income is too high for you to make a Roth IRA contribution as an unmarried taxpayer, you might be able to make a contribution as a married taxpayer. For example, consider Anne and Susan again. If they are unmarried, neither Anne nor Susan can contribute to Roth IRAs. Susan has no earned income, and Anne earns more than the maximum income limit (in 2015, it's $131,000) for a single taxpayer. If Anne and Susan marry, then their combined income of $150,000 is under the minimum income limit (in 2015, it's $183,000) for married couples. As a married couple, they are both permitted to make the maximum allowable contributions to their Roth IRAs.

In other cases, marriage may suddenly make both of you ineligible to contribute to a Roth IRA. Suppose that you and your partner, as an unmarried couple, are both near the upper income limit for single taxpayers and are able to contribute individually to Roth IRAs; however, if you were to marry and com-

bine your salaries, you may find yourselves above the Roth IRA contribution limits for married couples. Consider a different situation for Anne and Susan. Anne and Susan each earn $100,000. As an unmarried couple, they can both contribute fully to a Roth IRA, because they are each below the income limit for a single taxpayer (in 2015, it's $116,000). If they marry, their combined income would be $200,000. Marriage puts them above the 2015 phase-out limit of $193,000 for a married couple and prevents both of them from making any Roth IRA contributions at all.

To see how marriage may affect your ability to contribute to retirement plans, please review the tables on the following pages. These are the income limits for 2015, and they are generally indexed for inflation every year. Also note that the amount that you can contribute can never exceed your Modified Adjusted Gross Income.

Table 2.1
Traditional IRA:
If You Are NOT Covered by a Retirement Plan at Work

If Your Filing Status is:	*and Your Modified AGI is:*	*Then You Can Take....*
Single, or Head of Household or Qualifying Widow(er)	any amount	a full deduction up to $5,500 or $6,500 if 50 or older
Married Filing Jointly or Separately, Spouse Does Not Have a Plan at Work	any amount	a full deduction up to $5,500 or $6,500 if 50 or older
Married Filing Jointly, Spouse Does Have a Plan at Work	$183,000 or less	a full deduction up to $5,500 or $6,500 if 50 or older
	$183,001 - $192,999	a partial deduction
	$193,000 or more	no deduction
Married Filing Separately, Spouse Does Have a Plan at Work	less than $10,000	a partial deduction
	$10,000 or more	no deduction

Table 2.2
Traditional IRA:
If You Are ARE Covered by a Retirement Plan at Work

If Your Filing Status is:	and Your Modified AGI is:	Then You Can Take....
Single, or Head of Household	$61,000 or less	a full deduction up to $5,500 or $6,500 if 50 or older
	$61,001 - $70,999	a partial deduction
	$71,000 or more	no deduction
Married Filing Jointly, or Qualifying Widow(er)	$98,000 or less	a full deduction up to $5,500 or $6,500 if 50 or older
	$98,001 - $117,999	a partial deduction
	$118,000 or more	no deduction
Married Filing Separately	less than $10,000	a partial deduction
	$10,000 or more	no deduction

Table 2.3
Roth IRA: Allowable Contributions

If Your Filing Status is:	*and Your Modified AGI is:*	*Then You Can Contribute....*
Single, or Head of Household	less than $116,000	up to $5,500 or $6,500 if 50 or older
	$116,000 - $130,999	a reduced amount
	$131,000 or more	– $0 –
Married Filing Jointly, or Qualifying Widow(er)	less than $183,000	up to $5,500 or $6,500 if 50 or older
	$183,000 - $192,999	a reduced amount
	$193,000 or more	– $0 –
Married Filing Separately	less than $10,000	up to $5,500 or $6,500 if 50 or older
	$10,000 or more	a reduced amount

Finally, if your income exceeds the limitations for a Roth IRA, consider contributing to a nondeductible IRA. You can convert the nondeductible IRA to a Roth IRA the minute after you make the nondeductible IRA contribution. That is exactly what I do personally, in addition to my 401(k) contribution. For example, in January, I made both current and prior year nondeductible IRA contributions for me and my wife Cindy (even though she doesn't work outside the home). We converted our nondeductible IRAs to Roth IRAs, and, since we did it immediately, the tax due on the conversion was next to nothing. So, even though our household income is above the limit shown in the table above, we were able to put away a quick $26,000 tax-free into Roth IRAs ($6,500 each for 2014 and 2015), not including what I contributed to my 401(k).

Please note this conversion of nondeductible IRA to a Roth without incurring taxable income only works if you don't have any other traditional IRAs with basis. If you do have other traditional IRAs with basis, there is a rule that says you have to include their basis when calculating the taxable portion of the conversion. You should talk to your tax advisor about this strategy before you take advantage of it, because you could have a big surprise at tax time. But, for a taxpayer like me who has no other traditional IRAs with basis, this technique works very well. In effect, after the monkey business, it is just like making a Roth IRA contribution, but you have to do the monkey business first to get around the income limitations.

Because retirement plans allow your money to grow tax-deferred or tax-free, and we have already seen the enormous power of retirement plans, you may want to consider the impact that marriage will have on your ability to contribute to an IRA or a Roth IRA.

How Should You Plan for Your IRA and Retirement Plan After Your Death?

This is the part I really wanted to get to because this is where getting married vs. remaining unmarried makes an enormous difference.

I want your family and heirs to preserve the IRA and retirement plan for as long as possible after you die, employing the same concept as in the accumulation stage and the distribution stage, i.e., your spouse and/or your children should pay taxes later, even after you are gone. This is the third leg of my *"pay taxes later"* mantra. Again, assuming the family can afford it, I want them to withdraw only what they are required to withdraw from their inherited IRAs or retirement plans.

There are exceptions for Roth IRAs and Roth IRA conversions, but I will not go through that analysis here. Readers interested in Roth IRA contributions, Roth 401(k)s and Roth IRA conversions should read another one of my books, *The Roth Revolution, Pay Taxes Once and Never Again* (Morgan James, 2010).

Fundamentally, what I wanted to convey from this background section is that my *"pay taxes later"* premise is sound and you can rely on this concept and this advice.

The Tax Law for IRAs and Retirement Accounts as It Relates to Same-Sex Couples

The section below gets somewhat technical. But, before we get lost in a blaze of numbers and slightly difficult concepts, let's look at the big picture. There are significant opportunities for continued tax-deferral, or paying-taxes-later, for a married person who leaves his or her IRA or retirement plan to his or her surviving spouse. On the other hand, if you leave your IRA to your unmarried partner, the current law offers significantly less favorable opportunities for tax-deferral on an *Inherited IRA*.

An *Inherited IRA* is a unique asset for a non-spouse beneficiary—it is much different from an IRA that one spouse *inherits* from the other spouse. As unfair as it is right now for unmarried partners, anticipated changes to the tax laws regarding *Inherited IRAs* for unmarried individuals are expected to make tax acceleration on *Inherited IRAs* much worse. There will be loads more to pay in taxes if you are not married. (I have written at length about the *stretch IRA*—a way for non-spouse beneficiaries to defer income taxes on *Inherited IRAs*, but that is likely to be a disappearing tactic as a result of this anticipated change to the law.)

As of 2013, married same-sex couples are entitled to inherit their deceased spouse's IRAs or retirement plans and receive the benefits of that transaction. That means, if you are legally married and your spouse dies, you can treat his or her IRA as your own by rolling it into your IRA, or by designating yourself as the account owner. This is the same favorable tax treatment that straight couples have always enjoyed. If you are not legally married, then the likely prospect (after the anticipated change to the law) is a massive income tax acceleration on the *Inherited IRA* within five years of the death of your partner. (Please note: I am assuming that the *stretch IRA*, where the non-spouse beneficiary of an IRA can continue to defer taxes for their lifetime, will be overturned in the next several years.)

As shown in the analysis in the charts at the end of the chapter, if you *don't* plan appropriately, the difference between what your partner vs. your spouse could end up with could easily be measured in hundreds of thousands of dollars. Therefore, for financial reasons, if you are in a committed relationship, you hold a large IRA, and you are concerned about protecting your partner, consider getting married.

If you don't feel like grinding through the nitty-gritty analysis that follows this paragraph and you just want a quick view of the differences between getting married and implementing our advice vs. not getting married (which in the eyes of the IRS is: remaining "single"), please skip to the end of the chapter and look at all the graphs.

Down to the Nitty-Gritty

Prior to 2013, if the owner of an IRA or retirement plan died, the IRS treated their same-sex spouse beneficiary the same way they treated a non-spouse beneficiary, which, in short, is not nearly as favorable as the treatment for a spousal beneficiary. Now, when same-sex married IRA owners leave their IRAs to their spouses, the surviving spouses derive the same favorable results as straight couples. So, it is important to understand the difference between the way the IRS currently treats spousal beneficiaries and non-spousal beneficiaries, but perhaps it is more important to understand how the IRS will *likely* treat non-spousal beneficiaries in the future.

Who Can Inherit an IRA?

The individual beneficiaries for IRAs (both Roth and Traditional) can be divided into two basic categories:

- Spouse beneficiary
- Non-spouse beneficiary

First, it must be understood that the IRS does not permit you to leave money in tax-deferred retirement plans indefinitely—eventually, the money must be withdrawn from the plans. These mandatory withdrawals are called Required Minimum Distributions (RMD) or sometimes Minimum Required Distributions (MRD). Below is a summary of the current rules for IRAs and Roth IRAs for the owner and the two different types of beneficiaries.

- Roth IRAs

  1. Roth IRA Owner - no required minimum distribution for you.

  2. Spousal Beneficiary - no required minimum distribution for your spouse.

  3. Non-spouse Beneficiary - must take required minimum distributions beginning the year after the Roth IRA owner died, but the distributions are tax-free.

- IRAs

  1. IRA Owner - must begin to take minimum required distributions from their IRA in the year they turn age 70. (Technically, April 1 the year following the year you turn 70½, hereafter—for simplicity—70.)

  2. Spouse Beneficiary – a spouse who inherits an IRA can roll their spouse's IRA into his or her own IRA and delay RMDs until they turn age 70.

  3. Non-spouse Beneficiary (under current laws) – Must take minimum required distributions starting the year after the year of death of the original IRA owner.

If an unmarried person leaves his/her IRA to his/her partner (or anyone who is not his or her spouse for that matter), the beneficiary receives a *new type of asset* called an *Inherited IRA*—this is different from inheriting an IRA from your spouse.[3] Below are the key differences between an *Inherited IRA* and a *Spousal IRA:*

- *Spousal IRA*

  1. RMD start date – begin taking required minimum distributions after you turn 70.

  2. Life expectancy used for calculating RMD – Uniform Lifetime Table is used which yields a longer life expectancy and a lower RMD.

- *Inherited IRA* (under current laws)

  1. RMD start date – begin taking required minimum distributions right away (by December 31 of the year after the owner's death), regardless of your age.

  2. Life expectancy used for calculating RMD - Single Life Expectancy Table is used which yields a shorter life expectancy and a higher RMD, meaning significant income tax acceleration.

---

[3] In the past, when a same-sex partner was the beneficiary of an IRA he/she was treated as a non-spouse beneficiary. With the Supreme Court ruling, same-sex spouses can now enjoy the same benefits of Spousal IRAs that straight couples enjoy.

For an *Inherited IRA*, under the current laws, both the RMD start date and the life expectancy values combine to force you to accelerate your income taxes and deplete your *Inherited IRA* more quickly than with a *Spousal IRA*. As a result, with an *Inherited IRA*, less and less of your money grows tax-deferred, producing less money for you overall.

A non-spouse beneficiary of an IRA *cannot* roll an *Inherited IRA* into his or her own IRA. However, (under the current laws) the owner of an *Inherited IRA* still has some ability to defer the income tax on the account. The non-spousal beneficiary, assuming he does it right and wants to *"pay taxes later"* should only withdraw the RMD from the *Inherited IRA*. The distribution is calculated by dividing the amount of the *Inherited IRA* by a factor that represents the life expectancy of the beneficiary.[4]

A Case Study of a Same-Sex Couple

Reviewing Finances for Surviving Spouse if One Person Dies and Leaves His IRA to His Partner/Spouse

Doctor Dan and Baker Bob are in a committed relationship. For this scenario, Doctor Dan is 78 and Baker Bob is 72. Their incomes are quite different, with Doctor Dan providing the majority of financial support for the couple's needs. Right now, they are not married, and they live in Pennsylvania. In this section we will look at options for Doctor Dan's significant IRA.

Table 2.4 (on the following page) shows Doctor Dan's projected RMDs well beyond his realistic life expectancy. This table shows how long an IRA can be extended by the owner of the IRA if he or she limits withdrawals to his RMDs even though he will obviously not live to 116.

For our example, Doctor Dan dies at age 78, right after taking his distribution for that year! The balance in Doctor Dan's IRA is $1,000,000. Baker Bob, age 72, is his beneficiary. What are the different outcomes for that money based on whether or not Doctor Dan and Baker Bob get married or remain unmarried?

---

[4] The RMD is based on the beneficiary's life expectancy as of December 31st of the year following the year the IRA owner died. The life expectancy for different ages can be found in IRS publication 590.

Table 2.4
Doctor Dan's Projected Distributions from his IRA
(based on the IRS Table 3 – Uniform Lifetime)

Doctor Dan's Age	IRA Balance Beg of Yr ROR 6%	Life Expectancy	Required Minimum Distribution (Taxable)
78	$ 992,277	20.3	$ 48,881
79	$ 1,000,000	19.5	$ 51,282
80	$ 1,005,641	18.7	$ 53,778
81	$ 1,008,975	17.9	$ 56,367
82	$ 1,009,765	17.1	$ 59,051
83	$ 1,007,757	16.3	$ 61,826
84	$ 1,002,687	15.5	$ 64,689
111	$ 50,653	2.9	$ 17,467
112	$ 35,178	2.6	$ 13,530
113	$ 22,947	2.4	$ 9,561
114	$ 14,189	2.1	$ 6,757
115	$ 7,878	1.9	$ 4,146
Total Distributions			**$ 2,177,077**

Note: No consideration for inflation has been included in this table.

Outcome 1:
The Couple Remains Unmarried (Given Current Laws on Inherited IRAs)

As part of an unmarried couple when Doctor Dan dies, Baker Bob is now the owner of an *Inherited IRA*, and Baker Bob must use the Single Life Table (from IRS publication 590) to calculate his RMDs. Baker Bob's first distribution has to be withdrawn by December 31 of the year following Doctor Dan's death, and Baker Bob's life expectancy is calculated based on how old he will be at the time the withdrawal has to be completed. That means that Baker Bob will

Table 2.5
RMD's for Unmarried Baker Bob's Inherited IRA from Doctor Dan
(based on the IRS Single Life Table)

Baker Bob's Age	IRA Balance Beg of Yr ROR 6%	Life Expectancy	Required Minimum Distribution (Taxable)
73	$ 1,000,000	14.8	$ 67,568
74	$ 988,378	13.8	$ 71,622
75	$ 971,762	12.8	$ 75,919
76	$ 949,594	11.8	$ 80,474
77	$ 921,267	10.8	$ 85,303
78	$ 886,122	9.8	$ 90,421
79	$ 843,444	8.8	$ 95,846
80	$ 792,454	7.8	$ 101,597
81	$ 732,309	6.8	$ 107,692
82	$ 662,093	5.8	$ 114,154
83	$ 580,815	4.8	$ 121,003
84	$ 487,401	3.8	$ 128,263
85	$ 380,686	2.8	$ 135,959
86	$ 259,410	1.8	$ 144,117
87	$ 122,211	0.8	$ 122,211
88	$ -		$ -
	Total Distributions		**$1,542,149**

Note: No consideration for inflation has been included in this table.

be 73 when he has to make his first withdrawal, and his life expectancy is 14.8 years—the life expectancy of a 73-year old using the IRS Single Life Table. (Note: the Single Life Table is much less favorable than the Uniform Lifetime Table that Baker Bob would have been able to use had they been married.)

The RMD for the *Inherited IRA* is calculated by dividing the balance in the account as of December 31 of the year of death, by the life expectancy of the beneficiary. Assuming that the balance of the *Inherited IRA* was $1 million,

Baker Bob's first RMD would be $1 million divided by 14.8, or $67,568—which is fully taxable.[5]

This technique of limiting distributions from *Inherited IRAs* to the RMD is referred to as the *stretch IRA*. You stretch out distributions for as long as you can based on your life expectancy to minimize the tax acceleration on the money taken out of the account—which is the same as deferring taxes as long as possible. Let's look at Table 2.5 (on the previous page) to see what happens to the IRA if Doctor Dan and Baker Bob remain unmarried. The total distributions amount to $1,542,149 and the *Inherited IRA* is depleted when Baker Bob is 88 years old.

Outcome 2: The Couple Marries

Now, let's look at what would happen if Doctor Dan and Baker Bob were married. Baker Bob now has two options:

1. Treat the IRA as an Inherited IRA. (Wrong choice—distributions according to Table 2.5)

2. Treat the IRA as his own IRA, by doing one of the following (see Table 2.6 on the following page)

   • A Trustee-to-trustee transfer to his own existing or new IRA

   • A Spousal IRA rollover to his own existing or new IRA

Retitling Doctor Dan's IRA (the name on the account can just be changed, if you do not transfer the account to a new financial institution)

Table 2.6 reflects Baker Bob RMDs if he elects to roll Doctor Dan's IRA into his own IRA as a widowed spouse.[6,7] Instead of using the Single Life Expectancy Table that Baker Bob would have had to use had he been unmarried, Bob can now use the more favorable Uniform Lifetime Table to calculate his life expectancy. This table yields a life expectancy of 24.7 years in place of the 14.8 years that unmarried Baker Bob had to use. This longer life expectancy

---

[5] As they live in Pennsylvania, there is also the issue of inheritance taxes, but for our purposes we are assuming these taxes were paid with money from outside the IRA (which is what we recommend).

[6] All versions of "Treat the IRA as his own IRA" in option 2 above would effectively yield the same result.

[7] To simplify matters, we once again assume that Baker Bob has enough after tax assets to cover the 15% non-marital Pennsylvania Inheritance Tax that he would be required to pay.

Table 2.6
Baker Bob's Inherited IRA from Married Spouse

Baker Bob's Age	IRA Balance Beg of Yr ROR 6%	Life Expectancy	Required Minimum Distribution (Taxable)
73	$ 1,000,000	24.7	$ 40,486
74	$ 1,017,085	23.8	$ 42,735
75	$ 1,032,811	22.9	$ 45,101
76	$ 1,046,973	22.0	$ 47,590
77	$ 1,059,346	21.2	$ 49,969
78	$ 1,069,940	20.3	$ 52,706
110	$ 76,062	3.1	$ 24,536
111	$ 54,617	2.9	$ 18,834
112	$ 37,931	2.6	$ 14,589
113	$ 24,743	2.4	$ 10,309
114	$ 15,299	2.1	$ 7,285
115	$ 8,495	1.9	$ 4,471
	Total Distributions		**$2,573,350**

Note: No consideration for inflation has been included in this table.

will result in a smaller RMD and less taxes every year. That means more money can continue to stay invested in the tax-deferred IRA. And over the course of his life expectancy, married Baker Bob winds up with $1 million dollars more in total distributions than unmarried Bob, from the same IRA account. To be fair, we didn't include the time value of money, or inflation, or the reinvested money if Baker Bob has a higher minimum required distribution of the *Inherited IRA* than his spending needs. So, the value to Baker Bob is somewhat less than $1M, but it is a lot—sufficient for Doctor Dan and Baker Bob to consider getting married.

Not only does married Baker Bob have more money than unmarried Baker Bob, married Baker Bob's financial picture even outshines Doctor Dan's. Not only is the RMD smaller for married Bob than it is for unmarried Bob, but it is even smaller than it would have been for Baker Bob's husband, Doctor Dan. Because Baker Bob is younger than the doctor, his life expectancy factor is greater than Doctor Dan's: 24.7 years v 20.3 years. The longer life expectancy provides additional time for tax-deferred growth. Using the "stretch" gives Baker Bob an extra $400,000 (as compared to Doctor Dan, had he lived on) in distributions over the lifetime of the IRA that Bob inherited and rolled into his own account.

More Bad News if the Couple Remains Unmarried (Under Proposed Laws for Inherited IRAs)

Unfortunately, it looks like the extended tax and wealth accumulation benefits afforded by the "life expectancy" stretch for an *Inherited IRA* may soon go the way of the dinosaur. For several years, Congress has been looking for ways to reduce the benefits of an *Inherited "stretch" IRA*. To bring in more revenue, Congress is looking into imposing a finite term on the tax-deferred "stretch" of an *Inherited IRA*. The finite term that is being considered is five years, and many think the change will take effect within the next year or two. (For more on this topic see the "Proposed Regulation Changes" at the end of the chapter.) If this happens, an IRA beneficiary will have to withdraw the balance of the entire *Inherited IRA* by the end of the fifth year after the death of the original owner.

Table 2.7 assumes the proposed regulation changes will occur. This scenario spreads the distributions over all five years in an effort to minimize the income tax consequences of taking a large distribution all at once.

Let's Review the Numbers

As you can see when comparing all four tables, the longer the "stretch," the more financially beneficial it will be for you and your heirs.

- Table 2.4 represents the amount Doctor Dan would have received had he lived to age 115 and withdrew only the minimum from his IRA ($2,177,077). This is obviously unrealistic, but in order to be able to compare apples to apples, we had to run the projection for the same number of years.

- Table 2.5 assumes that Doctor Dan dies at age 78 and Baker Bob stretched the IRA for as long as he could (under the current law), considering that they never married. ($1,542,149)

Table 2.7
Unmarried Baker Bob's Inherited IRA 5 Year Distribution Limit

Baker Bob's Age	IRA Balance Beg of Yr ROR 6%	Year After Death	Tax-Wise Distribution 5 Yr Stretch
73	$1,000,000	1.0	$225,000
74	$821,500	2.0	$225,000
75	$632,290	3.0	$225,000
76	$431,727	4.0	$225,000
77	$219,131	5.0	$219,131
	Total Distributions		**$1,119,131**

Note: No consideration for inflation has been included in this table.

- Table 2.6 represents the stretch that Baker Bob can count on if he and Doctor Dan marry. When Doctor Dan dies at age 78, Bob rolls Dan's IRA into his own IRA and continues taking distributions based on his life expectancy (from the Uniform Life Expectancy table). ($2,573,350)

- Table 2.7 also assumes that the couple never marries, but this time the stretch is limited to the five years as we predict future law will require. ($1,119,131)

Comparing best to worst case scenarios (Table 2.6 to Table 2.7) Baker Bob would have an additional $700,000 by age 90 simply because the couple married prior to Doctor Dan's death. (The graphs later in this chapter will show you the growth of Baker Bob's net assets for the next generation.)

The Case Study Continues for the Second Generation of Heirs

Reviewing Finances for the Child of the Surviving Partner

Okay, now let's add another variable to the scenario. Imagine that Baker Bob adopted a child, Penniless Perry. Penniless Perry is their sole beneficiary after they both pass.

Outcome 1: The Couple Remains Unmarried with Penniless Perry (Given Current Laws on Inherited IRAs)

Both Baker Bob and Penniless Perry were heartbroken when Doctor Dan passed away. After Doctor Dan's death, the never-married Baker Bob began taking the required minimum distributions from the *Inherited IRA* that he received from Doctor Dan (Table 2.5). Only five short years later, Penniless Perry loses his adopted father, Baker Bob, at age 77.

As stated previously, Baker Bob had named Penniless Perry, his 50-year old son, as the beneficiary of the *Inherited IRA* (the one Baker Bob inherited from Doctor Dan—it gets a bit complicated, but stick with me). In this case, Penniless Perry is *required* to continue taking distributions from the *Inherited IRA* according to the calculations based on *Baker Bob's life expectancy*—not his own life expectancy.

Distributions from a second generation *Inherited IRA* are based on the previous beneficiary's life expectancy. This is the case when someone inherits an *Inherited IRA*. The IRS wants their tax revenue on the *Inherited IRA*, so they force Penniless Perry to continue taking distributions at Baker Bob's rate, despite Penniless Perry's longer life expectancy.

We know that Baker Bob took distributions from this account for five years. According to the *stretch IRA* schedule (Table 2.5), the balance left in the *Inherited IRA* when Baker Bob died at age 77 is $886,122. Penniless Perry's required minimum distribution is calculated by dividing the IRA balance of $886,122 by Baker Bob's initially projected life expectancy factor – or 9.8. This means that during the year after Baker Bob's death, Penniless Perry would be required to withdraw $90,421 from the IRA that he inherited from Baker Bob, who inherited it from Doctor Dan—and again, that's fully taxable. Table 2.8, on the next page, lists Penniless Perry's annual required distributions until nothing is left in the IRA.

If he only took the RMDs and nothing more, Penniless Perry would receive $1,161,263 in total distributions from his father, unmarried Baker Bob. The final payout from the *Inherited IRA* would occur when Perry is 87 years old. If you are keeping track, you will notice that Table 2.8 and Table 2.5 have the same life expectancy factor and distributions in the later years. That is because the current law requires Penniless Perry to treat the IRA exactly as his father had. Penniless Perry assumes the "life expectancy" of his father and must continue RMDs at the same rate as his father would have been required to, had he lived.

Table 2.8
Penniless Perry's RMD from the Second Generation Inherited IRA
(assuming that Doctor Dan and Baker Bob do NOT Marry)

Child's Age	Inherited IRA Beg Balance ROR 6%	Life Expectancy	Required Minimum Distribution (Taxable)
51	$886,122	9.8	$90,421
52	$843,444	8.8	$95,846
53	$792,454	7.8	$101,597
54	$732,309	6.8	$107,692
55	$662,093	5.8	$114,154
83	$580,815	4.8	$121,003
84	$487,401	3.8	$128,263
85	$380,686	2.8	$135,959
86	$259,410	1.8	$144,117
87	$122,211	0.8	$122,211
88	$0		$0
		Total Distributions	**$1,161,263**

Note: No consideration for inflation has been included in this table.

Outcome 2: The Couple Marries and Share Custody of Penniless Perry

Now, let's look at the same scenario with one critical difference: Doctor Dan and Baker Bob are married. What effect does this have on Penniless Perry's inheritance? Baker Bob is 72 years old when Doctor Dan dies and leaves him the IRA which is worth $1 million. Baker Bob wisely elects to treat the IRA as his own, and he lists Penniless Perry as the sole beneficiary. Since Baker Bob is age 72, he will be required to take RMDs from the IRA, but the distributions are based on the more favorable Uniform Lifetime Table. After five years of Baker Bob taking distributions, the IRA he inherited from his husband has a balance of $1,069,940 (much higher than in the previous example, because

Bob and Dan were married).[8] When Baker Bob dies at the end of the fifth year, Penniless Perry inherits the IRA from his father. Since his parents were married, Perry gets to "stretch" the *Inherited IRA*, taking required minimum distributions *based on his own (Perry's) life expectancy.*

Table 2.9
Penniless Perry's Inherited IRA Assuming Parents Married

Adult Child's Age	IRA Balance Beg of Yr ROR 6%	Life Expectancy	Required Minimum Distribution (Taxable)
51	$1,069,940	33.3	$32,130
52	$1,100,078	32.3	$34,058
53	$1,129,981	31.3	$36,102
54	$1,159,512	30.3	$38,268
55	$1,188,519	29.3	$40,564
56	$1,216,833	28.3	$42,998
80	$748,607	4.3	$174,095
81	$608,983	3.3	$184,540
82	$449,909	2.3	$195,613
83	$269,554	1.3	$207,349
84	$65,937	0.3	$65,937
85	$0	0.0	$0
	Total Distributions		**$3,193,608**

Note: No consideration for inflation has been included in this table.

Clearly, Penniless Perry will be much better off if his dads marry. Calculating his RMDs based on his own life expectancy allows his inheritance to continue to grow tax deferred for a much longer period of time. Compare

---

[8] Refer to Table 3 to see married Baker Bob's balance at age 77.

Tables 2.8 and 2.9. If Perry did nothing but collect his RMDs from his inheritance, under current law he would receive distributions for another 24 years if his fathers are married, resulting in total distributions of $3,193,608 instead of $1,161,263.

Further Complications for the Child if the Couple Remains Unmarried and the "Stretch" Laws Change

Table 2.10
Penniless Perry Second Generation Inherited IRA
from Unmarried Father – 5 Year Limited

Adult Child's Age	IRA Balance Beg of Yr ROR 6%	Years After Death	Tax-Wise Distribution 5 Yr Stretch
51	$886,122	1.0	$200,000
52	$727,289	2.0	$200,000
53	$558,926	3.0	$200,000
54	$380,462	4.0	$200,000
55	$191,290	5.0	$191,290
Total Distributions			**$991,290**

Note: No consideration for inflation has been included in this table.

If Congress changes the laws and enforces a five year distribution rule on *Inherited IRAs*, a marriage between Bob and Dan becomes even more important to Penniless Perry.[9] With the five year limit in place (not a given—currently just a threat), Penniless Perry would have to deplete the second generation *Inherited IRA* according to the five year rule, vs. the slower distribution schedule that would have allowed him to continue distributions based on his father's life expectancy—10 years. That would reduce what he would ultimately receive

---

[9] Assume, for this example, that Congress changes the law after Doctor Dan dies, but before Baker Bob dies. If the change is made before Doctor Dan dies, then Baker Bob will have depleted his Inherited IRA (see Table 2.7) and there would be no IRA for Perry to inherit.

by roughly $170,000 (Total Distributions from Table 2.8 minus Total Distributions from Table 2.10 on the previous page).

Table 2.11
Penniless Perry Second Generation Inherited IRA
Married Parents – Tax-Wise 5 Year Stretch

Adult Child's Age	IRA Balance Beg of Yr ROR 6%	Years After Death	Tax-Wise Distribution (Taxable)
51	$1,069,940	1.0	$240,000
52	$879,736	2.0	$240,000
53	$678,121	3.0	$240,000
54	$464,408	4.0	$240,000
55	$237,872	5.0	$237,872
	Total Distributions		**$1,197,872**

Note: No consideration for inflation has been included in this table.

If Dan and Bob had married, however, Bob could have stretched his distribution schedule for a longer period, which would mean that Perry's *Inherited IRA* would be greater ($1,069,940 vs. $886,122.) And, although the five-year distribution rule would still reduce his total distributions, he would still be better off by $206,585 (Total Distributions from Table 2.11 minus Total Distributions from Table 2.10).

Let's Summarize the Numbers for the Case Study

First, let's simply look at the finances for the couple.

We compiled the data from Tables 2.5, 2.6, and 2.7 and added a 6% Rate of Return and a 3% Rate of Inflation to generate the graph on the following page.[10] Had we used a higher Rate of Return, the differences would be far more dramatic. We can plainly see that Baker Bob will have more assets available for his retirement years, if he and Doctor Dan marry. Ten years from the date of his inheritance, married (and widowed) Baker Bob would have an additional

$94,000 in invested assets as compared to what he would have had if he had remained unmarried and stretched his *Inherited IRA*. The advantage of getting married becomes even greater the longer Baker Bob lives. When we look at unmarried Baker Bob under the anticipated law change, we see at age 90, married Baker Bob will have accumulated over $380,000 more than the unmarried Baker Bob, who had to deplete the IRA within five years. This puts him into a much higher tax bracket and significantly reduces his savings.

Figure 2.3
Inheriting an IRA from a Spouse vs. an Unmarried Partner

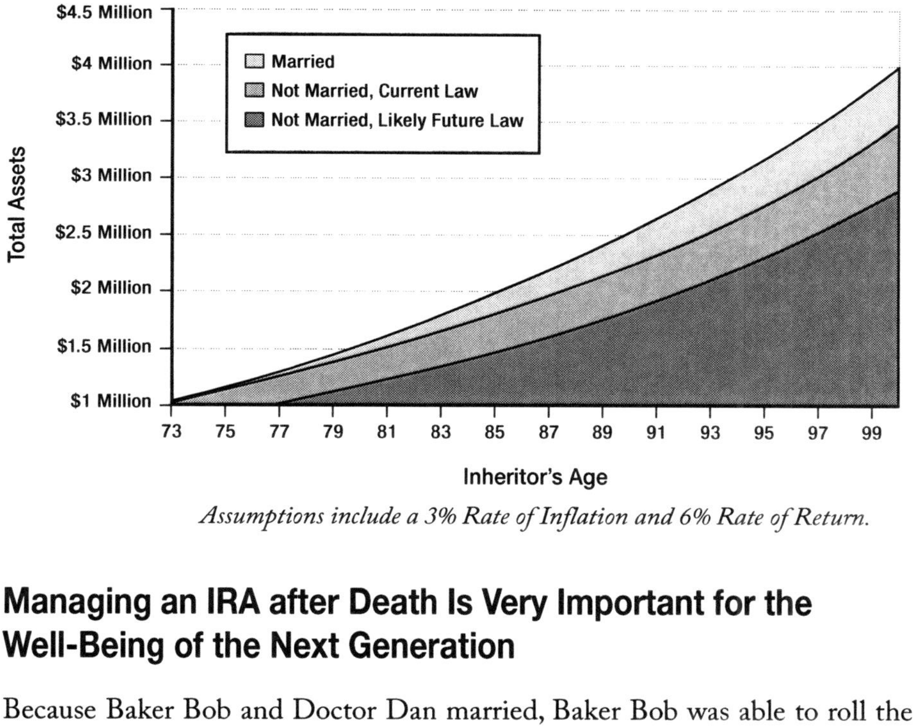

Assumptions include a 3% Rate of Inflation and 6% Rate of Return.

Managing an IRA after Death Is Very Important for the Well-Being of the Next Generation

Because Baker Bob and Doctor Dan married, Baker Bob was able to roll the IRA that he inherited from Doctor Dan into his own IRA account. In turn, this allowed Baker Bob's son, Penniless Perry, to calculate his RMDs based on

---

10 Although the RMD varies from one example to another, we assume that the living expenses will not vary. All money withdrawn from the IRA that is not needed for living expenses is assumed to be put into an after-tax investment and grows without tax-deferral.

Assumptions for Figure 2.3 and Figure 2.4 include a 6% Rate of Return and a 3% Rate of inflation.

his own life expectancy (as opposed to Baker Bob's life expectancy for a second generation *Inherited IRA*). Penniless Perry's *Inherited IRA* now grows tax deferred for a longer period of time.

The graph below includes Tables 2.8, 2.9, and 2.10 adjusted with a Rate of Return of 6% and an Inflation Rate of 3%. The difference in investment income from a married parent's IRA as opposed to an unmarried parent's IRA could amount to millions in additional income over Penniless Perry's lifetime.

Figure 2.4
Inheriting a Second Generation IRA from a
Married Parent vs. an Unmarried Parent

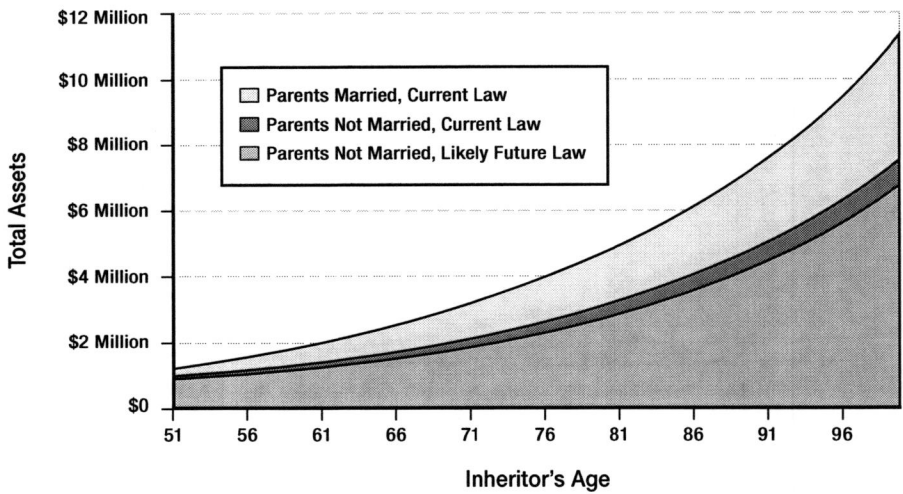

Assumptions include a 3% Rate of Inflation and 6% Rate of Return.

Just by getting married, Baker Bob is able to leave an additional $183,000 to Penniless Perry from the IRA he inherited from Doctor Dan and rolled into his own. Penniless Perry, son of married partners, also gets the benefit of an additional 24 to 29 year stretch because he can base his RMDs on his own life (first generation *Inherited IRA*) expectancy as opposed to the life expectancy of his unmarried father (second generation *Inherited IRA*).

Assuming that Penniless Perry reinvests all of his RMDs into after-tax investments, and that his father was married, he would earn additional income by age 60 of $1,830,046 v $1,113,549 if his father remained unmarried; by age 70 of $3,003,499 v $1,749,269; and age 80 of $4,682,296 v $2,747,918.

We could present this analysis in different ways using different assumptions. The conclusion will likely be the same. Same-sex couples with significant IRAs who are otherwise inclined to get married, should get married for the financial protection of the beneficiary of the IRA.

Well, you made it over the hump; you've accumulated well and planned for your retirement. What happens next? You need an estate plan for your heirs. Please picture yourself after the necessary changes have been made, knowing that you have set things up in the most beneficial manner for your family. If you marry, your spouse will be grateful with the gift of security you are providing. Imagine how good you'll feel knowing that you have to a large extent protected your estate from the IRS and got the most from your Social Security for you and your partner/spouse.

If you are already married and all of your documents are in great shape (and now after reading this book you will be in a better position to know), you should be applauded! If, however, things aren't in great shape or if you have questions, please read on and then take action so that your legacy won't be decimated by taxes.

Proposed Regulation Changes

As previously mentioned, it looks like the extended tax and wealth accumulation benefits afforded by the *stretch IRA* may soon go the way of the dinosaur. In 2012, Senate Finance Committee Chairman Max Baucus proposed limiting the *stretch IRA* to five-years-after-death for a non-spouse beneficiary, effectively making the beneficiary pay all the income taxes on the *Inherited IRA* over those five years. Thankfully, that proposal was withdrawn for lack of support. The idea reappeared, however, in April 2013 in President Obama's budget proposals, and made a grand entrance in the summer of 2013 when the measure was reintroduced as a part of a bill to reduce future student loan debt.

Killing the long benefit of the *stretch IRA*, they felt, would provide the revenue necessary to reduce student loan interest rates for college students, for one year. This bill was introduced in June of 2013 and died in the Senate with a vote of 51-49 in favor of another bill to reduce student loan interest rates. To be fair, the bill would have had a tougher time getting through the House, but President Obama wanted to sign it.

It is becoming increasingly clear that this measure, or a similar one, may eventually pass—some say as early as this year. I have had numerous discussions with top IRA experts in the country and everyone seems to agree that the *stretch IRA* as we know it now will likely be eliminated. On **The Lange Money Hour**, both Ed Slott, the best known IRA expert in the country, and Sy Goldberg, a politically connected IRA expert, said the stretch as we know it will not survive. (Please see **www.paytaxeslater.com** for the sound file and the transcript of those shows). Congress, in all its wisdom, has decided that forcing your non-spousal heirs to pay income taxes on your entire IRA or retirement plan within five years of your death will provide them (Congress) with a quick budget fix. Unfortunately, that fix will have sad consequences for your children or grandchildren. It will also have dire financial implications for same-sex couples who don't get married, where the large IRA owner predeceases the other partner.

Does this possible change in the law mean that you shouldn't bother investigating how a *stretch IRA* might benefit your estate plan? Of course not! A beneficiary who is your spouse will still retain the right to treat your IRA as his or her own – thus prolonging the "stretch" for his or her own lifetime. No one is proposing to change how the IRA will be treated if you name your spouse as the beneficiary. However, there could be serious consequences for a partner who is your IRA beneficiary, *but not your spouse*. For this reason alone, every committed same-sex couple should consider formal marriage to protect the spouse who is likely to inherit the retirement assets.

The line of demarcation will be the date of the IRA owner's death. If that individual dies before the legislation is passed, then their non-spouse beneficiary will get the stretch afforded by the Single Life Table discussed above. If the IRA owner dies after the proposed legislation is passed, their non-spouse beneficiary will have to pay tax on the entire account within five years. You can see that this legislation will have a significant impact on the finances of your non-spouse partner. If you want to receive updates on the status of these changes, please sign up for our newsletter at **www.outestateplanning.com**.

In the past, even if you understood the laws governing inheriting IRAs, you might not have factored them into your decision of whether or not to get married because the IRS treated your spouse or your partner as a non-spouse.

Well, all that has changed. It is very important that both you and your beneficiary understand how your options change when you become a legally recognized married couple.

The biggest action point in this chapter is that if you are not currently married but are in a committed long-term relationship, you should consider getting married. This is especially true if one of you has a large IRA or retirement plan that you want to leave to your partner.

Of course, all of this good advice about retirement plans becomes irrelevant if you do not stay married. Prenuptial agreements, as good as an idea as they may be, are not covered in this book. The specifics of handling pension plans in divorce are well beyond the scope of this book because, in general, the division of marital property is governed by the domestic relations laws of the state in which you live.

If you have married or are considering marriage, you should understand that a pension earned during a marriage is generally considered a joint asset of both spouses, and a court order (called a Domestic Relations Order) is necessary for an individual to receive a share of the spouse's pension. If a pension is divided between divorcing spouses, it generally must be done at the time of divorce—an important point because pensions can be easily overlooked if the divorce takes place years before retirement.

3

||||||||||||||||||||||

Same-Sex Couples and Social Security Benefits

Social Security is a promise that we cannot and must not break.

— Bernie Sanders

Main Topics

- Could the prospect of Social Security benefits influence our decision to legally marry?

- When should someone begin taking Social Security?

- What are some of the best strategies to maximize Social Security benefits?

> # KEY IDEA
> Perhaps the most important financial advantage of getting married is to increase your and your partner's/spouse's Social Security benefits for the rest of both of your lives and then the life of the survivor. The added value of the spousal benefit and the spousal survivor benefit are so important, those benefits might be a good enough reason to get married.

Significant Social Security Benefits for Married Couples

This chapter is one of the two most important and potentially life-changing chapters in this book. The other is Chapter 2 on IRAs and retirement plans. Why? Because they address some of the most compelling reasons to make good financial decisions for you and your partner's long-term financial security, including the decision of whether or not to get married.

The first idea to be explained in detail is that there are significant Social Security benefits for married couples, which are *not available* for two non-married partners. Up until 2013, the Social Security Administration did not recognize legal, state sanctioned same-sex marriages for the purpose of allowing Social Security benefits. Under the old law you were treated as two unmarried people—to your financial detriment. After the Windsor decision in 2013, the Social Security Administration agreed to allow spousal benefits only for same-sex couples who lived in states that recognized same-sex marriages. The subsequent decision of the Supreme Court now means that all legally married same-sex couples are eligible for spousal benefits from Social Security. This has created a financial planning bonanza for legally married same-sex couples! For couples that haven't yet taken the nuptial plunge, this could easily tip the scale toward getting married in order to enjoy enormous additional Social Security benefits. Let me give you an example.

The Big Picture

Imagine two identical couples – they are the same ages, they have the same assets, and the same earnings records. One couple gets married and takes advantage of the strategies recommended in this chapter. The other couple remains unmarried and both partners start collecting Social Security at age 62. Twenty years pass, and their lifestyles and spending remain identical. Eventually, the individual with the stronger earnings record of both couples dies. The financial situations of the two surviving partners is now drastically different: the survivor of the couple who got married and followed our advice has $400,000, the survivor of the couple that didn't get married, and chose to take Social Security early, is nearly broke.

The details follow later in this chapter. This example isolates the difference due to Social Security benefits. Granted, it is not likely to mirror anyone's situation exactly, but it does highlight the point that the Social Security spousal benefit alone may provide a compelling reason for same-sex couples to get married. For high-earning couples, or even more compellingly, when there is one higher-earning partner/spouse and one lower-earning partner/spouse, the value of the Social Security spousal benefit could potentially be measured in the hundreds of thousands of dollars (described below). One of the most important factors to consider is that, if the higher-earning spouse is the first to die, Social Security increases the monthly income for the lower-earning spouse following the death of the higher earning spouse. For couples of more modest means, the difference may not be as dramatic in terms of absolute numbers; nevertheless, getting married *and* taking the appropriate steps can provide a solid base for both of you in retirement during your joint lifetimes, and after the death of your spouse.

Unfortunately, sophisticated Social Security strategies are unfamiliar territory for same-sex couples, advisors to same-sex couples and even most financial advisors to straight couples. Granted, few straight couples know enough about the nuances of Social Security strategies to get the most from their benefits. But I do. In this chapter, I combine that knowledge with what I know about current laws affecting same-sex couples.

It is crucial to understand that there are multiple strategies for maximizing Social Security benefits, and that the vast majority of Social Security recipients—whatever their sexual orientation or marriage status—fail to apply any of these perfectly legal strategies to maximize their benefits. My objective here is to point out the advantages of spousal benefits for legally married same-sex couples, and to recommend strategies that will help you to get the most out of your Social Security benefits. Let me also add that decisions about whether or not it makes financial sense for you to get married, at what point you should collect Social Security benefits, and, to the extent that you have a choice, which

Social Security benefits you should collect, should not be considered in isolation. Because of the enormous financial implications that I'm about to show you, you should keep in mind that one decision will often have a consequence in a different area. For instance, did you know that there is an advantageous synergy that comes from combining the timing of Social Security benefits and making multiple Roth IRA conversions? Assuming you fit the profile (including being married), an advantageous Social Security election (described later in this chapter) combined with a series of Roth conversions starting after retirement, can make a significant difference in your financial security during your golden years. Above all, your personal situation, the personal situation of your partner/spouse, and your collective financial/retirement plans should all factor into your decision about how and when to claim Social Security benefits. My objective is to point out the advantages and disadvantages of some scenarios and hopefully motivate you to get more information for your particular circumstances—either on your own or with the help of an expert financial advisor.

Chapter Overview on Social Security

This chapter includes:

1. a summary of the critical features of Social Security benefits applicable to everyone who has either

   • paid into Social Security through payroll taxes and has worked long enough to have earned a benefit or

   • who is married to such a worker;

2. the current policy of the Social Security Administration regarding same-sex couples; and

3. strategies to maximize Social Security benefits.

This chapter also addresses:

1. how the options available to married couples that affect Social Security benefits might have an impressive impact on your decision to legally marry your partner;

2. how and why you both need to think about the timing of your application for Social Security benefits; and

3. whether it might be advantageous to use the *"Apply and Suspend"* technique we introduce in this chapter.

After the Windsor decision, the Social Security Administration needed time to revise their policies and procedures, and encouraged married same-sex couples to apply for spousal benefits even if they weren't sure that they would be eligible. The idea was that, if they were later determined to be eligible for spousal benefits, they would be granted retroactively. I disagree. The retroactive benefits might not be to your advantage—you don't know. I will give you the same advice I have been giving to straight couples for years: *don't apply for Social Security without thinking through your best strategy; you could do more harm than good.*

If you can't stand going through the details of the rest of this chapter, just skip to the end and read the recommended action points. Please, at least glance at Figure 3.2 *"Unmarried vs. Married Using Apply and Suspend for Social Security"* later on in the chapter.

The Basics

I'm going to begin by explaining the basics of Social Security benefits—and for now, we will forget about the marriage issue. One question I am always asked is this: "When is the best time to apply for Social Security benefits: as soon as you are eligible, several years later, or when you reach age 70?" Let's just talk about whether it makes sense, in general, to take Social Security as soon as you are eligible. For discussion's sake, let's assume your attitude is, "Well, gee, I'm retired, I'm 62 years old, I've been paying into this system for my whole life, and now it's time for me to get some money out." So you sign up and start receiving benefits. Should you have waited?

Comparison of Taking Social Security at Age 62 or Age 70

First, it is important to understand that the dollar amount of the benefit you will receive for the rest of your life depends upon the age at which you begin to collect it. Let's assume you were born between 1943 and 1954. Your full retirement age (FRA) is 66. This is set by law. The amount you will get if you begin to collect benefits at age 66 is called your Primary Insurance Amount (PIA). If you begin to collect benefits at a different age, the amount you will receive is a function of your PIA. If you begin early, you obviously start receiving an income earlier, but allowing for interest, etc. (details to follow), you will receive less per month than if you had waited. If you start taking benefits at 62, the earliest age at which you can begin to collect benefits, you will suffer the maximum reduction (25%) in benefits. If you begin to collect benefits after full retirement age, you will receive larger benefits. For every year you wait after your FRA, your Primary Insurance Amount will be increased by Delayed Retirement Credits that, as of this writing, accumulated at a rate of 8% every year. You can get the largest benefit by waiting until age 70, when your Delayed Retirement Credits increase your Primary Insurance Amount by a full 32%. So, the two extremes would be signing up for benefits at age 62, or waiting and taking Social Security at age 70. The earlier you collect, the lower your benefit will be for the rest of your life.

The following table shows the percentage of your PIA (the amount you would get at age 66) that you will receive if you begin to collect benefits early, and if you decide to delay. For every year that you wait to collect benefits after full retirement age (FRA) you will earn an extra 8% per year. Please note this chart doesn't include cost of living adjustments (COLA), which in all instances makes the advantages of waiting even greater.

Application Age		Benefits Received (% of PIA)
62		75.0%
63		80.0%
64		86.7%
65		93.3%
66	(FRA)	100%
67		108%
68		116%
69		124%
70		132%

FRA = Full Retirement Age

Running the Numbers for a Single Social Security Recipient

To accurately compare the financial benefits of waiting until age 70 to apply for benefits, vs. collecting them at age 62, we are going to assume that you will not spend any of your benefits from the time you start collecting until the time you reach age 70. In fact, we are going to assume that you will reinvest all the benefits you've received, until age 70. If we don't make that assumption, it is extremely difficult to make an "apples to apples" comparison.

For our example, we have two single people with identical earnings records. One starts collecting his benefits at age 62 and invests all of his benefits at a 6% rate of return. The other person waits until age 70 to begin collecting.

Figure 3.1

Starting Social Security Benefits at 62 Years Old vs. 70 Years Old

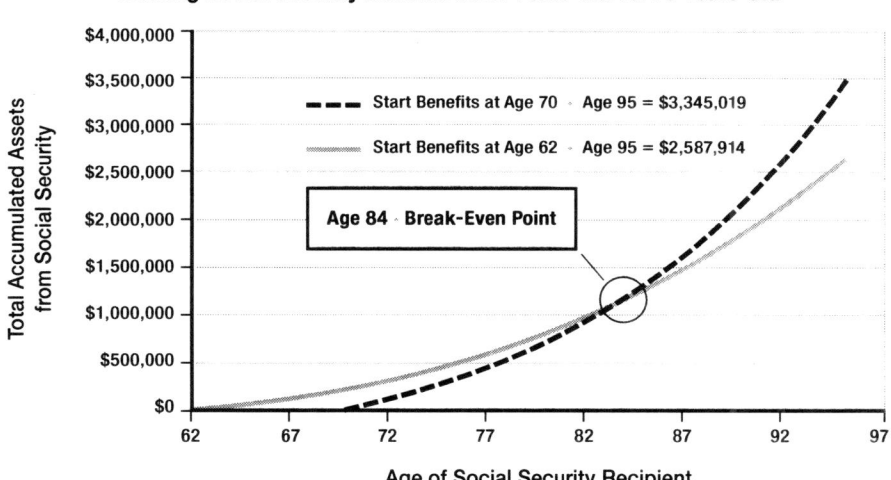

The solid line in Figure 3.1 above represents the money accumulated over time by the individual who started collecting his benefits at age 62, and the dashed line represents the money accumulated over time for the one who waited until age 70 to begin taking benefits. The graph shows that the person who waits until age 70 to take Social Security will ultimately receive a lot more in benefits than the person who takes the benefit at age 62, assuming that he or she lives long enough (age 84 is roughly the breakeven point). The graph assumes a 6% rate of return. If you assume a lower rate of return, the breakeven age would be even younger.

If you take benefits at 62, you will receive 75% of what you would have received if you waited until age 66 (your PIA). If you wait until age 70 to apply, you will receive 132% of what you would have received had you taken benefits at age 66 (or an additional 8% per year). This means that, if you wait until age 70 to apply, there will be a 76% increase in your monthly benefit over what you would have received if you applied at age 62. (The math here may not be immediately obvious so, consider an example. If your PIA at 66 is $100, and you decide to apply for benefits at age 62 you will get $75. If you wait until 70, you will get $132. The additional amount that you would get for waiting is $57 [$132-$75 = $57]. The percentage by which you will have increased your benefit is 76% [$57/$75].)

You might think that age 84 is a long time to wait to break even, and you might even wonder if you're going to live long enough to realize the benefit of waiting. But, here is why you should consider waiting. You may think the conservative thing to do is to take it early because if you don't survive to age 84 you will "win." That is the way I used to think about it until I was enlightened.

Larry Kotlikoff, an economist at Boston University, and a guest on **The Lange Money Hour**, taught me a better way to think about it.[1] "Don't think like an actuary," declares Larry, "think like an economist." You have to think about what you *should* be afraid of and what you *should not* be afraid of, from a financial perspective. From a financial perspective, you should not fear an early death. You will be dead, and therefore you will have no more financial problems. *Your biggest fear should be not having enough money comfortably support a long life.* When you delay collecting Social Security for as long as possible, you ensure a greater income into your old age.

In our example, if you live to age 95, the difference, in terms of the total amount collected, would be $3,345,019 vs. $2,587,914. That's more than $750,000 additional dollars in your own pocket. The key concept to understand is this: the longer you live, the bigger the difference in the amount you collect and the greater your financial security if you live a long time. Let's face it, if you begin taking benefits at age 62 and you don't absolutely need them, and you die shortly thereafter…well, you are dead. No more worries. "But wait," you say, "what about my spouse who is still alive? I want to take care of him/her too." Exactly.

---

[1] I have a radio show, The Lange Money Hour, and I talk with the top experts in the areas of retirement and estate planning and investments. Larry was a guest on the show when he enlightened me. There are115 hours of archived shows, including transcripts, which are available at **www.paytaxeslater.com**.

Remember, in our example we are only talking about an individual who is *not* married. As will be seen, marriage introduces a completely new set of concerns that make waiting longer to collect benefits even more lucrative and financially secure. Yes, there is certainly a chance that the Social Security Administration will change its policy in a way that is disadvantageous to you. However, every knowledgeable person I have spoken to about this issue, including Larry Kotlikoff, who is pretty tuned-in politically, says that the risks of taking Social Security benefits early far outweigh the risks of significant reductions for people who are currently age 62 or older.

You should rest assured. You are going to get Social Security benefits as long as you are alive.

— Bill Bradley

Delay Claiming Benefits to Provide Long-Term Security for Your Surviving Spouse

Although spousal benefits will be discussed in greater detail later in the chapter, one point that needs to be understood immediately is that, typically, the surviving spouse is going to receive benefits based on the higher of the two earnings records. So, if you are the higher earner in the family, and you hold off applying for benefits until age 66 or 70, (as opposed to collecting at age 62), you not only create a higher benefit for the rest of your life, but you also protect your lower earning surviving spouse in the event that you predecease him or her. This is an extremely important idea, and may even be seen by some as so critical for protecting the lower-earning spouse, that this fact alone may justify getting married. If the objective is to have enough money to live comfortably for the rest of both of your lives, then the person with the stronger earnings record will usually be well advised to wait to apply for benefits.

Scenario 1: Married Couple, Surviving Spouse Collects Survivor Benefit

Let's assume that the spouse with the stronger earnings record waits until age 70 to collect benefits, and her benefit grows to $3,000/month. Let's also assume that her lower earning spouse has a $2,000/month benefit of her own based on her lower earnings record. The spouse with the stronger earnings record then dies. Even though the surviving spouse's benefit based on her own earnings record is only $2,000/month, she can claim the full amount of her deceased spouse's benefit (which would be the $3,000/month) after her death. This assumes that the surviving spouse has reached her full retirement age of 66. Calculating the survivor benefit can be more complicated if the survivor hasn't reached full retirement age, or if the deceased spouse claimed benefits before her full retirement age.

Scenario 2: Unmarried Couple, No Survivor Benefit for Surviving Partner

The couple in question is not married, but they receive the same income from Social Security as the couple in the previous example: the lower-earner's benefit is $2,000/month and the higher-earner's benefit is $3,000/month. Then the higher-earning partner dies. The surviving partner will continue to receive her own $2,000 /month. The other partner's benefits stop when she dies. No survivor benefit is paid to the surviving unmarried partner.

The ability of the lower earner to take a survivor benefit if the stronger earner dies first could mean the difference between the survivor being broke and being marginally okay, assuming that the couple did not have a significant amount of other assets. This is especially true if there is a big difference between the higher earner's benefit and the lower earner's benefit. The issue of protecting the partner with the lower earnings record is critical. Providing for the lower-earning spouse, in my opinion, should weigh heavily in the decision of when the spouse with the stronger earnings record should begin collecting Social Security benefits. It is not just an individual issue—it is a family issue.

I am not alone in endorsing the general concept of the higher-earning spouse holding off on collecting Social Security. I am only applying a well-documented (but not generally known) concept from the straight couple world to the same-sex couple world. Four guests from **The Lange Money Hour**, all experts in their respective fields, have all gone on the record as saying that the spouse with the stronger earnings record should wait at least until age 66, but probably until age 70, to start collecting Social Security, not just to protect themselves, but to protect the surviving spouse.[2] The four experts who are in agreement on this concept are:

- Jane Bryant Quinn, one of the top financial writers in the country

- Mary Beth Franklin, former editor of *Kiplinger's Personal Finance Magazine*

- Larry Kotlikoff, economist, Boston University and author of *Get*

---

[2] Again, all these shows are archived, with a transcript, and are available at **www.paytaxeslater.com**.

What's Yours: The Secrets to Maxing Out Your Social Security,

- Kathleen Sindell, author, *Social Security: Maximize Your Benefits*

All the experts and authors mentioned above (including me) hate to see situations where the spouse with the stronger earnings record begins to collect at age 62. Waiting to start collecting Social Security is probably even more important for women (who generally have longer life expectancies) and for couples whose income after retirement is mostly or entirely made up of Social Security benefits.

Coming Out Later in Life and Protecting Your Partner

When Sue, a lesbian, was young, she began a traditional life, married a man and had children. She came out after her husband died, and now has a female partner. She is very connected to her children and grandchildren. Though she wants to provide for her partner, she feels compelled to leave her children and grandchildren all of her money, much of which came from her deceased husband's retirement plan. With her estate attorney, she drafts wills, trusts, IRA beneficiary designations, etc., leaving everything to a combination of her children and grandchildren.

Taking my advice, she waited until age 70 to begin collecting Social Security benefits on her own earnings record and now has a benefit of $3,000/month.[3] Her new partner has a benefit of $1,000/month, is retired and can't go back to work, and has no other financial resources. If Sue does nothing and dies, her partner will continue to get $1,000/month from Social Security and, unless something unexpected happens, will spend the rest of her life in dire poverty. If Sue marries her partner (and they sign an effective pre-nuptial agreement), Sue can still leave her children and grandchildren all her money

The difference is that her spouse (formerly her partner) would become eligible to collect a spousal benefit (spousal benefits will be explained later in this chapter) during their joint lives ($1,500 if she is full retirement age), and a survivor benefit at Sue's death ($3,000 if she is full retirement age). $3,000/month is a lot better than $1,000/month. The great thing here is that the increase didn't cost Sue, or Sue's children or grandchildren, one nickel.

---

[3] To keep this illustration simple, we're assuming that Sue was married to her husband for less than ten years. If they had been married for more than ten years, Sue might be better off collecting spousal benefits based on his earnings record. This topic is beyond the scope of this book, but if you were married previously, it is helpful to know that this could be an option for you.

If you are divorced, you may be eligible for Social Security benefits based on your ex-spouse's earnings record. There are also some stunning strategies where previous and current spouses can collect on the same high-earner's record, but that is beyond the scope of this book. Nevertheless, if you were married previously, you should pursue this idea with the appropriate expert. In the words of one divorced client who "got rid of her husband" then found out she could collect on his Social Security earnings record: "Finally, the no good S.O.B. is good for something!"

Strategies to Maximize Social Security Benefits

I will begin by telling you the one resource that you *should not* use to identify the best benefits strategy for you. Do not use the person who works for the Social Security Administration as your Social Security expert. That person is not likely a long-term strategic thinker. He or she is hopefully capable when it comes to providing you with information about your earnings record and your estimated benefit amounts, and for processing your application. Unfortunately, his or her expertise is unlikely to extend to Social Security planning, and most likely won't extend to planning for your overall financial well-being in retirement. I want to scream when I hear, "Oh, I know you told me to hold off on collecting Social Security but the person at the Social Security office said I should start collecting at 62. That's like taking the advice of the teller at the bank who says you should buy an annuity, instead of taking the advice of the CPA/Attorney with 30 years of finance experience who says you are you better off investing in a portfolio of well-diversified index funds.

The person who works for Social Security is not likely to be the person you want to use for strategic decision making. To be fair, there are some smart, capable people who work for the Social Security Administration, who may be able to give you sophisticated retirement and estate planning advice regarding your Social Security options, but I would not count on that person being the one who processes your application.

The goal for most married couples (whether same-sex or opposite-sex) is to identify and, if appropriate, collect the maximum Social Security benefits available for their lifetime and, ultimately, the remaining lifetime of the surviving spouse. Because spousal and survivor benefits are only available to married couples, any strategy in which spousal and/or survivor benefits are collected will result in cumulative benefits that exceed those available to single people. A strategy such as the *Apply and Suspend* strategy discussed below is only available to certain married couples. It maximizes both survivor benefits *and* benefits during the couple's joint life times, and demonstrates a compelling reason for same-sex couples otherwise inclined, to strongly consider marriage.

Spousal Benefits

A spousal benefit is a Social Security benefit paid to someone based upon their spouse's earning history. You can receive Social Security based upon your own earning history, or, if you have reached full retirement age, you can choose to receive a spousal benefit (50% of your spouse's benefit when your spouse turned 66). The lower wage earner can often collect a higher Social Security benefit based upon their spouse's earnings record than they can based on their own. The higher wage earner's monthly benefit is not affected in any way. The lower wage earner is eligible to collect more, simply because they are married. Generally, spousal benefits are available during a couple's joint lifetimes. Consider the following example:

Sue and Mary are the same age and they recently married. Sue has a $2,500/month benefit at age 66. Mary, her spouse, on her own earnings record, has a $1,000/month benefit at age 66. At age 66, Sue can collect her $2,500 benefit. Instead of the $1,000/month benefit due to Mary based on her own earnings record, Mary can collect $1,250 (half of Sue's $2,500) per month as a spousal benefit.

Using the Apply and Suspend Strategy to Enhance Cumulative Benefits

My favorite Social Security strategy involves one spouse, usually the one with the stronger earnings record, *applying* for, and then *suspending* collection of his or her benefits: the stronger earning spouse applies for Social Security benefits, and then suspends benefits until age 70. What is the difference between doing *Apply and Suspend* at 66 and simply waiting until age 70 to collect? For the person applying and suspending, there is no difference. But, by applying and suspending, you allow your spouse to collect spousal benefits *based on your earnings record*.

Now this is the fun part. In this situation, since neither individual will be collecting benefits based on his or her own earnings records, both individuals will continue to earn credit that will enhance their own benefits if and when they do begin to collect on their own records. In other words, the advantages of waiting to collect Social Security that were discussed earlier will still apply to both spouses, even though one of the spouses is collecting a spousal benefit based on the other spouse's earnings record. Here's how it works:

When the higher earner turns 66, she applies for Social Security and then immediately suspends her benefits. The lower earner can then file a *restricted* application for Social Security benefits (applying for spousal benefits, but not all of the Social Security benefits that this spouse is entitled to). From ages 66 to 70, the lower earner can collect this spousal benefit. In the meantime, the benefits for both spouses continue to grow, just as if neither of the two had collected any Social Security benefits at all. When the lower earner reaches 70, she is then able to choose between the Social Security benefit based upon her own earnings, or she can continue to receive the spousal benefit, obviously she will choose whichever is greater. Even though she was collecting a spousal benefit between age 66 and 70, her own personal benefit was not reduced and actually continued to grow – up to 32% – as if she had not claimed a nickel. At age 70, the higher earner "unsuspends" her benefits and begins collecting her Social Security. Claiming a spousal benefit does not impact the earnings record or the allowable benefits for either of the spouses. So, in addition to strengthening both benefits by four years, there is a "free" four-year spousal benefit. Full retirement age must be reached before an individual can suspend collection of his or her benefits and the spouse collecting the benefits must also have reached FRA. Again, full retirement age is age 66 for people born between 1943 and 1954. I have no idea why the government decided to allow married Social Security recipients to be treated so generously. Maybe someday they will change it, but right now, this can be a grand strategy for many married couples.

While it can be an enormously beneficial strategy, it won't work for everyone. The spouses' ages and circumstances must be "right" in several ways. There are other strategies that could be even more advantageous than this one, based on your particular circumstances. The point of this chapter is not to give an exhaustive analysis of every Social Security strategy. Instead, the point is to show there are extremely advantageous strategies that you should know about and consider when planning your retirement finances and even the decision to get married. As I said earlier, much will depend upon your personal circumstances.

If you are interested in learning more about your Social Security options, I strongly recommend that you read *Get What's Yours: The Secrets to Maxing Out Your Social Security*, by Larry Kotlikoff, Philip Moeller, and Paul Solman.

Should the Apply and Suspend Technique Factor into a Decision to Get Married?

Let's revisit our friends Doctor Dan and Baker Bob. Dan and Bob are the same age and deciding whether it would be financially beneficial to marry. Both men would like to retire at the age of 62. Together, they have combined assets worth approximately $1,100,000. The couple estimates that their current annual living expenses are around $75,000 (increased annually for cost of living). During every year of his career, Doctor Dan earned the maximum amount that "counts" for Social Security. Knowing this, we can estimate the benefit he would receive if he began collecting at age 62, age 66 and age 70. In real life, his Primary Insurance Amount will increase for inflation each year. But for purposes of this discussion, we are going to say that the amounts he can receive as a high wage earner are $23,422 (75% of his Primary Insurance Amount if he collects early), $31,232 (his Primary Insurance Amount), and $41,226 (his benefit including Delayed Retirement Credits) per year respectively. During every year of his career, Baker Bob earned far less than Doctor Dan. Assume for this example that the benefit Baker Bob would receive if he began collect-

Figure 3.2

Unmarried vs. Married Using Apply & Suspend for Social Security

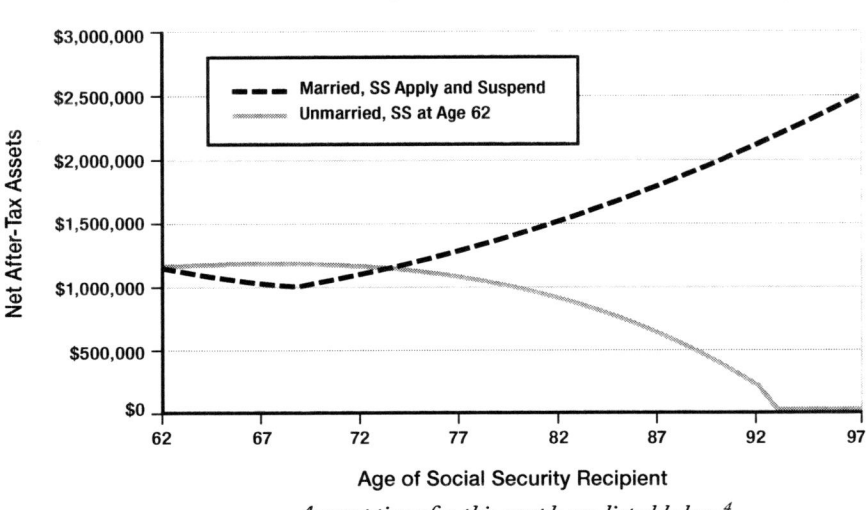

Assumptions for this graph are listed below.[4]

ing at age 62, 66 and 70 are $5,000, $6,667, and $9,070 per year respectively. Doctor Dan's goals are:

1. retire immediately, and

2. make sure that funds are available to support himself and Baker Bob until the end of both of their lives.

The following scenarios paint different pictures for collecting Social Security benefits.

1. The couple remains unmarried and they each collect their Social Security benefits at the age of 62. Baker Bob would receive $5,000 in benefits and Doctor Dan would receive $23,422 in benefits. As their

---

[4] 1. Starting date of projection is the year both partners turn 62.

2. Doctor Dan starts with $1,100,000 in after tax assets. Baker Bob starts with $50,000 in after tax assets.

3. Includes a 6% Rate of Return.

4. Includes an allowance for 3% inflation of expenses, tax brackets, and Social Security.

5. Annual living expenses are $70,000 for Doctor Dan and $5,000 for Baker Bob (plus income taxes).

6. In the single scenario, Doctor Dan receives $23,422 in Social Security benefits, Baker Bob receives $5,000. Both men begin benefits at age 62, and the benefits are increased annually for COLAs.

7. In the married scenario, Doctor Dan receives maximum Social Security benefits of $41,226 at age 70 plus COLAs, Baker Bob receives 15,616 at age 66 (½ of Doctor Dan's benefits at age 66) plus COLAs.

Figure 3.3
Unmarried vs. Married Using Social Security Apply & Suspend with an Early Death

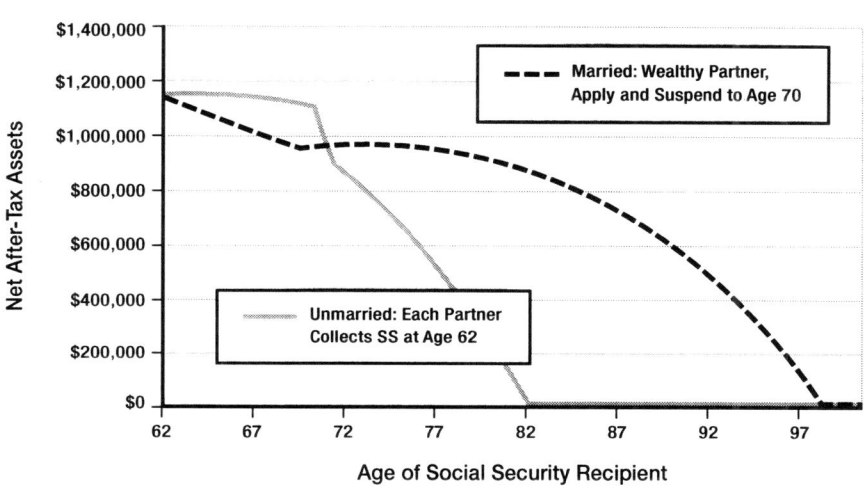

Assumptions for this graph are listed below.[5]

trusted advisor, I would not recommend that they retire at age 62 given their spending, but the client wants to retire now.

2. The couple gets married. Since this couple has other money available for living expenses, they follow my recommendation and do not collect Social Security benefits upon retirement at age 62. Instead, Doctor Dan applies for his benefits at age 66 and suspends them until age 70. Baker Bob can then claim the spousal benefit of one-half of Doctor Dan's benefits, or $15,616, starting when Baker Bob is age 66. This is much higher than Baker Bob's own benefit, which would be $6,667 at that time. Because he has waited, Doctor Dan's benefits will grow by the

---

[5] 1. Starting date of projection is the year both partners turn 62.

2. Includes a 6% Rate of Return.

3. Includes an allowance for 3% inflation of expenses, tax brackets, and Social Security.

4. Annual living expenses are $75,000, adjusted annually.

5. Doctor Dan dies at age 70 and leaves all his wealth to Baker Bob.

6. The current PA Inheritance Tax rate is 15% for the unmarried couple.

7. In the single scenario, Doctor Dan receives $23,422 at age 62, Baker Bob, $5,000 at age 62.

8. In the married scenario, Doctor Dan receives maximum Social Security benefits of $41,226 at age 70 plus COLAs. Baker Bob holds off taking a spousal benefit until age 66. He then receives ½ of what Doctor Dan would have received at age 66 or $15,616 (½ times $31,232.) plus COLAs. After Doctor Dan dies, Baker Bob receives survivor benefits of $41,226 plus COLAs.

8% delayed retirement credit per year from 66 to 70, plus cost of living increases until he turns 70, thus increasing the money available to care for both of them in their later years.

Figure 3.2 illustrates the difference in their assets had they remained single and collected at 62 versus getting married and using the *Apply and Suspend* strategy. But if both partners are alive at age 80, the difference in their net worth will be over $440,000. If they both live to be 90, the difference in their net worth will be over 1.5 million dollars. And that difference is a result of the couple tying the knot, and taking advantage of a technique that the Social Security Administration only makes available to married couples.

Now, let's imagine a worst case scenario. Both Doctor Dan and Baker Bob have drafted wills, trusts, beneficiary designations of IRAs, retirement plans, etc. saying that if something were to happen to one of them the other would inherit all the assets. Then, Doctor Dan, who used to keep his patients waiting for hours, develops cancer and dies…while waiting in the office of his oncologist. Baker Bob inherits all of Doctor Dan's assets. How long those assets will last is very different, depending on whether they married and use *Apply and Suspend* versus both taking their Social Security at age 62.

Just because the men chose to get married and use the *Apply and Suspend* technique, Baker Bob has enough money to last his entire lifetime.

The dashed line in the Figure 3.3 shows how much money will be available to care for Baker Bob if the couple remains unmarried, each takes his Social Security early, and Doctor Dan dies at age 70. If he doesn't marry, and doesn't change his spending habits, Baker Bob will run out of money at the age of 82.

The solid line represents Baker Bob's prospects if they get married and use the *Apply and Suspend* strategy. Baker Bob will most likely have enough assets to last his lifetime. Another factor to consider is your own state inheritance tax. For example, in my home state of Pennsylvania there is a 15% tax if you leave your money to your partner but no tax if you leave your money to your spouse. The inheritance tax rates of each state vary significantly, and are beyond the scope of this book to discuss in detail.

Ultimately, it would seem that the best financial strategy for Doctor Dan and Baker Bob would be to get married, delay Social Security benefits until age 66, and then use the *Apply and Suspend* strategy. Doctor Dan should also consider doing a series of Roth IRA conversions starting at age 62. While Roth IRA conversions are beyond the scope of this book, there are enormous benefits to doing a series of Roth IRA conversions while you are in a lower tax bracket.

Here is a summary of the basic *Apply and Suspend* technique:

1. At full retirement age, 66, the higher-earning spouse applies for Social Security benefits and then suspends collection.

2. The lower-earning spouse (also at full retirement age) applies for a spousal benefit.

3. At age 70, the higher-earning spouse will "un-suspend" and apply for his or her own benefit.

4. At age 70, the lower-earning spouse will either continue to collect the spousal benefit he or she has been receiving since age 66, or switch to his or her own benefit, depending on which is greater.

(As mentioned earlier, calculating the spousal benefit is more complicated if the lower earning spouse has not yet reached age 66, or if the stronger earning spouse had starting collecting before reaching 66.)

An Alternative Strategy: Claim Now, Claim More Later

There is also an alternative strategy to *Apply and Suspend*, in which the person with the stronger earnings record applies for a spousal benefit based on the record of the lower-earning spouse, then applies for the benefit on his/her own earnings record later (at age 70, for the maximum benefit) in order to accrue delayed retirement credits on his/her own benefit. This strategy may produce a better result than *Apply and Suspend*, depending on the relative ages of the spouses. That is also beyond the scope of this book, but it would be worth seeking the advice of a professional if you want to learn more about maximizing the benefits you receive from Social Security.

Summary of the Key Points and 5 Strategies You Can Use To Maximize Your Social Security Benefits

The key points to remember when deciding on the timing of applying for Social Security benefits are:

1. If you apply early, your monthly benefit starts lower *and* stays lower for life.

2. Cost of living adjustments (COLA) will magnify the impact of early or delayed benefits.

3. The longer you live, the more beneficial it will be to delay benefits.

4. Your decision to apply early or later impacts survivor benefits as well as lifetime benefits; delaying benefits may give your surviving spouse more income.

5. Spousal benefits must be taken into consideration.

There are five strategies that you can use to maximize your Social Security benefits and maximize your purchasing power. They are:

1. Improve your earnings record

2. Apply for Social Security at the optimal time

3. Coordinate spousal benefits, including the *Apply and Suspend* strategy

4. Minimize taxes on your benefits

5. Coordinate your Social Security benefits with other financial decisions and strategies

Let's discuss these strategies one at a time.

1. Improve Your Earnings Record

If you have already earned income up to, or exceeding, the Social Security wage base for 35 years, continuing to work may increase your benefit some-what, but the increase is not likely to be substantial. If you have not been a maximum earner for 35 years, working longer will make a significant differ-ence in your monthly benefit. The longer you work, the stronger your earnings record is going to be. I hate it when people who enjoy their work retire early so that they can get a benefit earlier. That doesn't make sense. If you like what you're doing, keep working—ultimately that's more money for you and for your spouse! I genuinely hope that all of you enjoy good health and live until a ripe old age, and it is my goal to make sure you have sufficient money to enjoy your retirement.

2. Apply for Social Security at the Optimal Time

To figure out the optimal time to apply for Social Security, you must take into account your income needs, both now and in the future, your life expectancy, and your spouse's life expectancy. Suzanne, a 62 year old retiree, has a serious health problem that causes her to believe she is *not* going to make it until age 84, the theoretical "breakeven" age for Social Security using the assumptions above. She may think that she'll be lucky to make it to age 72. If she is single and not planning on getting married, Suzanne should probably apply for Social Security benefits at age 62. But, if she is married and has the stronger earnings record, she might want to wait to collect her benefits to ensure that her surviving spouse will get the higher benefit. Suzanne's health, marital status, and estimated life expectancy are all very important parts of her analysis. What is your genetic factor? How long did your parents live? These are important questions to ask. While in general I recommend holding off, particularly for married people, sometimes it does make sense to collect early.

3. Coordinate Your Spousal Benefits to Produce Free Money

Consider whether you can use the *Apply and Suspend* strategy or the *Claim Now, Claim More Later* strategy at your full retirement age to produce "free money" over the years from age 66 to age 70.

4. Minimize the Taxation of Your Benefits – Always a Good Idea

There are different tax-planning techniques that will enable you to minimize income tax and also get the maximum enjoyment from your Social Security benefits. For example, even just holding off on Social Security benefits until after you're retired may keep you in a lower tax bracket. It may also produce a window of opportunity for annual Roth IRA conversions between the time you are retired and no longer receiving a paycheck, and when you turn age 70. Holding off on Social Security during those years will give you an opportunity to make larger Roth IRA conversions while you are in the lower tax brackets. Then, at age 70, when there is no advantage in holding off on Social Security, you collect the maximum benefit and you have also succeeded in making Roth IRA conversions while in the lowest tax bracket you will be in for the rest of your life. This assumes you have a substantial traditional IRA and will have to start taking minimum required distributions at age 70½. Once again, I recommend seeking the advice of a professional to coordinate Social Security and Roth IRA conversions. But it might be difficult to find a professional who really understands enough of the concepts to effectively "run the numbers." This is a niche that we have cultivated and take pride in doing well.

5. Coordinate Your Social Security Benefits with Your Overall Retirement Income Plan

Earlier in this chapter, I made the point that Social Security shouldn't be considered in a vacuum. There are many interrelated parts of a good financial plan. I like to integrate everything: a Social Security plan, an IRA plan, a long-term Roth IRA conversion plan, a general tax plan, an estate plan, and an investment plan. You must also take into account everything else that is going on, such as your pensions, your IRAs, your 401(k), your minimum required distributions, your working income, and your investment portfolio, and even the timing of when you should get married. What you don't want to do is to have an independent strategy for each piece of the puzzle. You want a synergistic strategy that incorporates all parts of your financial plan in concert with your life plans. And, this chapter provides compelling support for the proposition that committed same-sex couples in their sixties or older should likely get married to dramatically increase their financial security with Social Security during both of their lifetimes and after the first death.

Do you have a trusted advisor to help you with your retirement and estate planning? Do you feel confident he or she is qualified and experienced in the unique strategies that benefit same-sex couples? Is your current advisor well versed in the interplay between Social Security, retirement plan distributions, and Roth conversions? If so, great. Please, finish reading this book, list your comments and concerns, and set up an appointment as soon as possible.

If, however, you don't have a trusted advisor and can't find anyone that you feel has the appropriate expertise in integrating Social Security planning with retirement and estate planning specifically for same-sex couples, there is another option for some number of private clients who will work with me directly. I am offering a number of free consultations for qualifying residents of Western PA and taking on a very limited number of private clients who will work with me directly. I am also offering a number of paid consultations to non-Western PA residents. If you are interested in working with me and/or my firm one on one, please visit www.OutEstatePlanning.com/workwithjim or refer to the end of the book for contact information.

4

||||||||||||||||||||||||

Income Tax Changes for Married Same-Sex Couples

Anyone may arrange his affairs so that his taxes shall be as low as possible; he is not bound to choose that pattern which best pays the treasury. There is not even a patriotic duty to increase one's taxes.[1]

— Judge Learned Hand

Main Topics

- How marriage can affect the rate at which your income is taxed.

- How marriage can affect your eligibility for certain tax benefits.

---

[1] I recently saw my college roommate, a tax attorney who fights for the other side. He worked for the IRS. and now the Ohio Department of Revenue. He hates this quote.

> # KEY IDEA
>
> Marriage can have a significant impact on the amount of income tax you will owe, as well as any tax benefits that you might be eligible for.

How the Federal Income Tax Has Changed for Married Same-Sex Couples

Starting in tax year 2013, same-sex couples legally married in a state, or a foreign country, that recognizes same-sex marriage were required to file their federal income tax return as "married filing jointly" or "married filing separately." If you are married on December 31st, for income tax purposes you will be considered married for the entire year. *This only applies to couples who are legally married.*

If you tied the knot before you read this book, here are some things that you should think about. First, if you are an employee who must file IRS Form W-4, Employee's Withholding Allowance Certificate, you should review the W-4 on file with your employer. Your filing status and total number of allowances claimed may have changed for federal tax purposes.

Second, you should have your accountant review your federal income tax return to see how it will be affected. Here are some points to remember:

- Your standard deduction will change because the deduction is based on your filing status.

- Some income, deductions, expenses, and credits may change because of your new filing status.

- Your married filing status may change your eligibility for the Earned Income Tax Credit, Child Tax Care Credit, and subsidies for health care as well.

- Income tax treatment of employer-provided health insurance and fringe benefits will be different now that you are considered married for federal tax purposes. If you purchased same-sex spouse health coverage benefits or fringe benefits that were provided by your employer, those are now excludable from federal taxable income based on your marital status. That is great news. Not only that, if you paid tax on those benefits in the past, it might make sense to file an amended return to claim a credit or refund. Please see Chapter 6 for a review of health care concerns.

- If you or your new spouse is collecting Social Security benefits, your benefits may be taxed, or if they are already taxed, taxed at an even higher rate. This is because your household income will presumably be higher.

- You might potentially have the ability to take an additional tax deduction if you make a deductible IRA contribution on behalf of your spouse.

Consult your CPA or tax advisor to determine how these and any other changes based on your new filing status may affect you and your spouse. If you are a do-it-yourselfer, I find the easiest ways to test different scenarios is with tax software like Turbo Tax or Tax Cut.

Legally married same-sex couples who filed their federal tax returns as single may choose to file amended federal tax returns for one or more prior tax years, depending upon the statute of limitations. Generally, the statute of limitations for filing an amended return is three years from the date the original return was filed, or two years from the date the tax was paid, whichever is later.

If you are thinking of filing amended returns, we strongly recommend that you first "run the numbers" for married filing jointly versus filing as two single taxpayers, and/or have a discussion as soon as possible with your CPA or tax attorney. Then, depending upon the result, either you or your CPA could file amended returns and request any applicable refund. Filing amended returns is optional, and some couples might actually owe additional taxes to the IRS for previous years if they file amended returns reflecting a married status.

The Advantages and Disadvantages of Marriage on Your Federal Income Tax Return

Will there be federal income tax benefits to you if you get married? Unfortunately, there is no longer a "one-size-fits-all" answer to that question. If you

and your partner have highly divergent incomes, marriage may be beneficial. But, for many couples with dual high wages, your income taxes could actually increase if you get married because of the so called "marriage penalty" that currently hurts many straight couples. So, when is it good to get married for federal income tax purposes, and when will there be a marriage penalty?

Examples of the Marriage Bonus from Filing Jointly

If you have significantly different incomes, it is usually going to work out better to file "married filing jointly" as opposed to two single returns—a marriage bonus. The lower earner is helping to reduce the tax bracket of the higher earner, and that could save you a couple thousand dollars.

1. If you earn $80,000 and your spouse earns $20,000, and you file "married filing jointly" as opposed to filing single, you will save about $2,700 in income taxes.

2. If you earn $100,000 and your spouse does not work, and you file "married filing jointly" as opposed to filing single, you will save about $6,700 in income taxes.

Another benefit of marriage is related to the Net Investment Tax. The income threshold for married taxpayers is higher than the threshold for single taxpayers. So, if one of you has significant investment income and the other does not, marriage could cause a decrease in the Net Investment Tax that the higher earner owes.

Example of the Marriage Penalty from Filing Jointly

On the other hand, let's say that you both make about the same amount of money, and you are both high-earners. The marriage penalty usually comes into play when you have two relatively equal earners. The marriage penalty could be a difference of $1,000 or $2,000, or it could be as much as $4,000 or $5,000, depending on your combined income. And you will pay this increased amount of income taxes every single year, which can really add up to a large sum of money.

1. If you and your spouse each earn $150,000, and you file "married filing jointly," you will pay more in income taxes than if you had remained unmarried and each of you filed as "single."

Maybe Marriage is a Good Idea if you are Selling Your House

Another reason to get married and file jointly is if you are planning to sell your house, and the sale will result in a significant gain. If you are married, you get a $500,000 exemption from the capital gain, but if you are single, the exemption is only $250,000. So, if you're going to sell your house at a large profit you will be financially better off if you are married. You must meet ownership and use tests and must not have excluded gain from another home in the past two years.

Marriage Offers More Options for Retirement Plan Contributions

One very good reason to marry is that the IRS permits you to contribute to retirement plans on behalf of your spouse, even if he or she does not work. To make an IRA contribution for your spouse, he or she must be under age 70 ½ in the year for which the contribution is being made. And if you do not participate in an employer-sponsored retirement plan such as a 401(k) at work, you may be able to deduct the full amount of your spouse's IRA contribution. The income limits for deducting a traditional IRA change every year. And, even if you are not able to deduct contributions made to your own traditional IRA, you might be able to contribute to a Roth IRA instead.

Your Age Might Also Factor into Your Decision

The financial advantages and disadvantages of getting married will depend upon your particular circumstances—notice the word *financial* (that is the limit of my advice!). For example, if you are a relatively young couple, the disadvantage of the marriage penalty on your income taxes might be more important to you than the Social Security and the IRA beneficiary and estate planning advantages. (See Chapter 2 for IRAs and Chapter 3 for Social Security.) On the other hand, if you are a couple in your sixties, when Social Security and estate planning become more important to you, then your particular circumstances may weigh more heavily toward getting married. We tend to work with older couples, where the advantages of the increased Social Security benefits and the much more advantageous rules regarding inheritance of IRAs and retirement plans are more compelling than any tax increases. That will obviously not be the case for everyone.

Marriage and Your Social Security Benefits

Married or single, higher income taxpayers may have to pay income tax on a portion of their Social Security benefits. The amount of Social Security that is subject to tax depends on your income, but up to 85% of your benefits can be taxable. In order to determine whether or not your benefits are taxed, you have to add one half of your Social Security benefits, plus any non-taxable interest, to your adjusted gross income. If the sum exceeds the income threshold (which, as of this writing, is $34,000 for single people and $44,000 for married couples) up to 85% of your benefits may be taxable. So if your partner currently pays little or no income tax because most of his income is from Social Security, marriage may not be financially favorable if you file a joint return and your own income is higher than the threshold. Unfortunately, marrying and filing separate tax return will not help this problem because the married filing separately tax rates are so high.

Further Financial Considerations to Have on Your Radar

Let's assume you decide to get married because of the financial benefits described in this book. Does that mean you should get married tomorrow? What if you are thinking about a Roth IRA conversion? It might be better to do a Roth IRA conversion before you get married, in some circumstances. In others, it would be more advantageous to do a conversion after getting married. In many if not most cases, it will pay to start Roth IRA conversions for the stronger spouse after marriage, and start the financially weaker spouse's Roth IRA conversion before getting married. [For more on Roth IRA conversions see my book, *The Roth Revolution: Pay Taxes Once and Never Again.* (Morgan James, 2010)]

What Is Your Filing Status for State Income Tax Purposes?

Federal income tax returns calculate federal adjusted gross income (AGI) and federal taxable income, and these calculations take your filing status into account to determine your taxable income. Many states incorporate the federal amounts for adjusted gross income or taxable income into their state income tax returns. In addition, some states allow you to file separately even if you are married, and others require that you file jointly. Each state has its own rules related to filing status, so it's important to consult a tax professional to understand how your marriage status will affect your state tax return.

You will likely hear a lot about the income tax changes for same-sex couples in the coming months and even years. We have tried to cover some of the critical income tax issues in this chapter. Please remember, however, for most couples, income tax avoidance or reduction (unless you count income taxes on IRA distributions after death) is not the main financial motivation to get married. The main financial motivation for most same-sex couples to get married will be the treatment of IRAs and retirement plans at death and optimizing your benefits from Social Security.

5

||||||||||||||||||||||

Trusts for
Same-Sex Couples

Love all, trust a few, do wrong to none.

— William Shakespeare

Main Topics

- How to use a trust to protect loved ones.

- The potential downfalls of using a trust.

KEY IDEA

Attorneys love to set up trusts and they are not always appropriate. In most cases, my preference is to rely heavily on the trust that you have obviously placed in your spouse.

In this chapter, we present some traditional trust ideas as well as controversial alternatives to trusts. If trusts are appropriate, many same-sex couples should consider some variation of the total return trust as part of their estate plan.

There is no simple answer to the question of whether using a trust in an estate plan makes sense. Their appropriateness will depend upon your situation and the nature of your relationship. But, there are some cutting-edge techniques discussed below that can be used to address some of these perplexing questions.

Providing For Your Partner or Spouse after You Die While Still Protecting Your Own Beneficiaries (Who Are Not Necessarily the Same People as Your Partner's Beneficiaries)

A number of my clients do not share the same beneficiaries. One partner[1] might have a child from a prior marriage or relationship. Maybe neither partner has a child, and each would like their own families—brothers and sisters, nieces and nephews etc.—to be their eventual beneficiaries. And yet, your first level of concern is providing for your surviving partner or spouse. What do you do in that situation? Well, you could provide for your partner in your will, or name him as the primary beneficiary of your IRA[2] or life insurance, and then name members of your biological family as secondary (contingent) ben-

---

[1] Rather than complicate the explanations by saying "partner or spouse" throughout, I will simply say "partner." But be assured that these strategies work whether or not you are married to your life partner.

[2] It is the beneficiary designation of your retirement accounts and of your life insurance policy (and not your will) that establishes who will inherit these assets.

eficiaries. However, if your partner is still alive when you die with this simple designation, he or she will inherit everything. This is because the secondary beneficiary designation is a Plan B. The simple designation says that your partner would be your first choice to receive the money, but if he or she isn't alive when you die, then your second choice would be your family members. In this example, your partner was alive when you died, so there was no need to look any further. Your partner inherits all of your money, and your biological family receives nothing.

Now it will be your partner's will and beneficiary designations that control all of your money. After he or she dies, the potential exists for all of the assets that you left your partner to go to your partner's beneficiaries—not to your biological family or the particular charities that you may have wanted to provide for.

For example, let's say that the money you have now was inherited from your parents when they died, and their expressed intent was for that money to eventually be passed down to members of your biological family (their other children, or their beloved grandchildren). They would not mind providing for your partner, but they would much prefer that, after your partner dies, whatever is left should go to your family, not your partner's family. You agree, and want to honor their wishes. If you use the simple beneficiary designation mentioned above, with your partner as number one and your biological family as number two, your partner controls your family's money upon your death—which was never your intention. The standard solution is to create a trust, and make the trust your beneficiary.

How a Standard Trust Works

What are the terms of a standard trust? Usually it will be set up to say, "income to spouse, or income to partner, and at partner's death, the principal (whatever is left) returns to the biological family." Let's look at an example.

Let's assume Margie has a million dollars and she tells her attorney that if she dies first, she wants to make sure that her partner Jean is provided for. But after Jean dies, she wants the million dollars, or whatever is left of it, to go back to her younger brother Robert—and definitely not to Jean's daughter, who has never bothered to hide her dislike for Margie. The attorney prepares a legal document called a testamentary trust, which means that the trust is a part of Margie's will. It remains unfunded and does not take effect until the time of Margie's death. The terms of the trust say that Jean will get the income from the million dollars for as long as she lives. So at Margie's death, Jean does not receive the million dollars outright. The money goes to a trustee that Margie had chosen previously, and it is invested for Jean's benefit and, ultimately, for the benefit of her younger brother Robert. While Jean is alive, she will receive income from the trust, and then when she dies the corpus (or whatever is left) will return to Margie's brother Robert. It is important to note that neither Jean nor Robert can receive money at a faster rate than what Margie has specified in her trust. So if Jean receives her income as defined by the trust, but wants an additional $40,000 to buy a new car, she would be out of luck unless there was a provision in the will that specifically allowed her to receive more than just the income from the trust.

How a Traditional Trust Defines Income

So is naming a trust as your beneficiary a bad thing? Well, there can be some interesting complications with the standard trust, and those complications come from the way that most trusts define the word *income*. And this problem is even worse when interest rates are low. Traditionally, when trusts are drafted by attorneys, the word *income* is defined as "the interest and dividends on stocks and bonds or cash investment accounts."

What is usually missing in the standard language of a trust is any reference to "capital gains" or "appreciation." Currently, the interest rate on many bank accounts is maybe 1% to 2%, and dividends on many investments are not much higher. Let's assume that the trustee that Margie chose invested her million dollars in CDs at a local bank, and the CDs paid 2% interest. If the attorney who drafted Margie's trust used the standard definition of income, her partner might only receive $20,000 ($1 million x 2%) from the trust every year. That amount of money is not really going to do a great job of providing for Margie's partner, especially if she has no other sources of income. Yet when Jean dies, Margie's brother Robert will receive $1 million.

Suppose that the trustee that Margie chose invested most of the $1 million in a well-diversified portfolio of index funds, and the portfolio has grown to $2 million. Very little of the portfolio is invested in CDs, so Jean's income— just the interest and dividends—will not increase significantly and may not even keep pace with inflation. At Jean's death, though, Margie's brother Robert will receive millions from her trust. Margie's beloved partner Jean will not benefit from the significant gains in the stock market because the traditional definition of "income" as used in her trust does not include *appreciation*.

Use a Different Definition to Define Income

So, what can you do? If you like the idea of a trust, but you are concerned about meeting your partner's income needs, one solution is to redefine *income*. When drafting the trust, we can drop the traditional accounting definition of income (which is "interest and dividends") and use a definition that makes more sense for your intentions. Instead, we specify that our definition of *income* means *a percentage of principal.* And that can be 4% of principal, 5% of principal, or whatever percentage seems appropriate.

For this example, we will use a *4% of principal* scenario. We draft a trust for Margie that says, "At my death, my million dollars goes into a trust. My trust will pay 4% of the principal every year, to my partner Jean. When Jean dies, the corpus, or the principal of the trust, is returned to my brother Robert."

It is important to understand that, because of the trust, Margie's partner Jean does not have access to the million dollars when Margie dies. If the principal in the trust the first year is $1,000,000, Jean will only receive $40,000 from the trust (4% x $1,000,000). And, because we're defining income as a percentage of principal in Margie's trust, Jean's income will likely fluctuate from year to year.

Now, hopefully the trustee that Margie has chosen invests the million dollars wisely, for growth and appreciation. If the trust grows to $2 million, her partner's annual income from the trust would be $80,000 (4% x $2,000,000). If things turn sour and the trust assets decline to $800,000, then her surviving partner's income would drop to $32,000 (4% * $800,000). Either way, the outcome is more favorable for Jean than if Margie had used the standard definition of "income" for her trust. There are also formulas that could be used to "smooth" the annual distribution of income.

A Concept Called the Total Return Trust

As much as I might like to take credit for it, redefining income from "interest and dividends" to "a percentage of the principal" (or some variation thereof) was not my idea. Actually, one of the pioneers of this type of trust is an attorney in Pittsburgh, named Robert Wolf. Either he or somebody else dubbed it a "total return trust." Bob Wolf devised this concept at a time when interest rates were much higher. The challenge facing the trustees at the time was how to invest the money in the trust. If the trustee invested in assets that produced the most income (interest and dividends) possible, the income beneficiaries of the trust were happy, but the end beneficiaries weren't happy because the assets in the trust were not growing—meaning that they'd ultimately inherit less money. If the trustee invested for growth, the end beneficiaries were very happy because the trust assets they stood to inherit were increasing, but the income beneficiaries were furious because they didn't get very much money at all (remember, appreciation is not included in the standard definition of "income"). Wolf's solution, which I think was brilliant, was to define income as a percentage of principal.

Total return trusts have enjoyed tremendous growth with more enlightened law firms and banks and trust companies, though perhaps not as much as Bob Wolf would like. I borrowed Wolf's concept and applied it to my clients who were in same-sex relationships. In 2002, I put up a website called **www. outestateplanning.com** and wrote an article explaining why this concept was a good idea for same-sex couples.

Back then, there were different reasons to use the total return trust concept. Interest rates were much higher at the time, and the trustee was being helped with a total return trust because he could satisfy both the income beneficiaries and the end beneficiaries at the same time. Now, the total return trust concept is especially important to the income beneficiary because income, in the traditional definition, is just so bad in today's low interest rate environment.

Avoiding Conflict among Beneficiaries and Other Issues

A total return trust avoids conflict between the trustee, the ultimate beneficiary, and the life-income beneficiary. With a traditional trust, there are often arguments, even lawsuits, among the various beneficiaries and the trustee over how the trust assets should be invested. Even if interest rates do increase dramatically in the next few years, you still might have some of those same conflicts between the parties of a traditional trust. The income beneficiary might want the trustee to invest for income, and the end beneficiary might want the trustee to invest for growth—and the trustee is stuck in the middle because he or she can never make everybody happy.

However, if everybody has the same goal, i.e. growing the principal of the trust, *everyone* benefits. The income beneficiary will get more money, the end beneficiary will get more money, and the trustee, if his or her fee is based on how much money they are managing, will also get more money. It seems to be a win-win-win situation.

There are certainly many same-sex couples who should consider some variation of the total return trust as part of their estate plan, but trusts are not always appropriate or needed.

A Simple Solution When You Want to Provide for Your Partner and Others Heirs

A different solution, though not necessarily the best solution, is to leave either specific assets, or a percentage of your assets, to your partner/spouse. The remainder goes to your other heirs.[3] For example, you could leave your Roth IRA to your younger heirs , and your after-tax investment accounts to your partner/spouse. The problem with doing this might be that, if, after time passes, you spend all of your after-tax dollars, saving your Roth IRA dollars to spend last, your children will still inherit your Roth IRA but your partner will inherit nothing. The solution to that problem is to leave certain percentages of all your assets to your partner, and the remaining percent to your family or other heirs.

Life Insurance

Even if you or your attorney has the wisdom of King Solomon, sometimes there is no great answer to how you should divide up your estate between your partner or spouse, and your other heirs. This is particularly true when your partner is currently relying on your income, but your estate isn't big enough to provide for both your partner and your other heirs no matter how you slice up the pie.

Rather than sweating over the details of dividing up the pie, another simple solution is to just make a bigger pie—with life insurance! Life insurance is uncomplicated – there are no names to change on accounts, there are no assets to sell—it can make your partner and your other heirs happy. The only unhappy one is you, since you have to pay the premium.

And, while we are on the subject of life insurance, even if you are not trying to figure out how to divide the pie, sometimes life insurance is just appropriate to provide for your partner. Even if you are leaving your entire estate to your

---

[3] The idea of leaving your Roth IRA to your young heirs is to extend tax-free growth for as long as possible. However, if the government changes the laws for Inherited Roth IRAs, this may be no longer as relevant. In that case, if you are married, your marriage will allow for a longer period of tax-free growth for your spouse than it would for your partner.

partner, if your partner doesn't have sufficient assets to live comfortably even after inheriting your estate, you should consider making a bigger pie with life insurance.

Providing for Your Partner without Extended Family Constraints

What if providing for your partner is your primary concern?

The total return trust that I wrote about in 2002 on **www.outestateplanning.com** was not as popular with same-sex couples as I expected. Why? It turns out that most of my clients in same-sex relationships were primarily interested in providing for their partner, and what happened after the death of the second partner was not of great concern to them. Although a total return trust is a great idea for some couples, it doesn't necessarily make sense for others. For example, what if your entire estate is $300,000 instead of a million dollars? In that case, the income from the trust, no matter how you define it, is not going to be sufficient. Also, what if you want to plan for the unexpected after the first death? What if your partner needs more money because of health issues or if other unanticipated expenses arise?

One solution, but perhaps not the best solution, would be to change the terms of the trust. You could include language in your trust that says, "The trustee is authorized to invade the corpus of the trust for medical emergencies." Or, you could say, "The trustee is authorized to invade the corpus of the trust for health, maintenance, and support." This solution, although viable, is still not perfect, particularly for a smaller estate that will incur the costs and aggravation of trust administration. When you create a trust, there must be a trustee, perhaps a bank, perhaps a person, but in either case there will be additional tax returns, not to mention the cost of drafting the trust. Do you really want more bankers, lawyers, and accountants to get their greedy paws on your hard earned money instead of your partner? Is there an alternative to a trust?

An Alternative Solution is an Agreement with Your Partner

In this next section, I present the minority viewpoint and concede the majority may very well be right in many if not most cases. I present my view anyway, because for the right couple, maybe you and your partner or spouse, it can make an enormous difference and be the best estate plan there is for you.

Let's assume your *primary* concern is to provide for your partner—and if there is something left, you would like it to return to your biological family. But you don't want to do a total return trust because you don't think the income provisions, no matter how they are defined, will provide enough income for your partner. Plus, you don't like the idea of having to choose a trustee, and the taxes and the expenses of the trust are just added complications that you'd prefer to not deal with. And you also learned in Chapter 2 that it can be an unmitigated income tax disaster if you are married, and the asset that you wanted to put in your trust, is your IRA. Let's assume you also don't like the idea of splitting your estate in terms of percentages because you fear that, if it is less than 100%, you won't sufficiently be providing for your partner.

What about a different idea? Let's assume, for the sake of discussion, that you trust your partner unconditionally. (Not everybody does by the way—so if you don't, you are not alone and this solution will not work for you.) But if you do trust your partner, how about saying this to them?

> *"Here's the deal: I'm going to leave you all of my money (or at least a big chunk of it), but I want you to keep it in a separate account after I die. You're allowed to go into that account when you need it for your own purposes or for your own support, but you keep your own money in a separate account. Legally, all of the money will be yours. But our agreement* will be that you will agree to have a clause in your will and beneficiary designations, etc. that stipulates that, whatever remains of the money that I left you, which you have been keeping in a separate account, will be returned to my biological heirs or other heirs of my choosing upon your death."*

**A written agreement might add a bit of comfort.*

By having an oral or written agreement with your partner, you don't incur all the complications of the requirements of a formal trust. This includes the legal considerations and cost of drafting the trust, the need for a trustee after death, the extra trust income tax return, the extra complications for the beneficiaries who have to deal with a K-1 on their own tax return, and other aggravations and legal problems of a trust. You can keep things simple, but you can only do this if you *really trust* your partner. I have done this quite a bit in my practice and I will tell you that, with the exception of one time, it worked beautifully. To be fair, I have done this more with straight couples in a second marriage who are providing for their second spouse, but having the second spouse agree to provide for the children of the first marriage upon their death.

An oral agreement could work, but a written agreement gives greater, though not even close to perfect, assurance your partner will follow your wishes after you die. The written agreement is better if, for no other reason, just to make clear what the agreement is. But, whether it is written or oral, you must trust your partner to do as you ask.

There are estate attorneys, most likely the majority of estate attorneys, who would say I am crazy to even mention these types of agreements as an option—especially an oral agreement. They would say you can't trust anyone; after a death, *things* happen. I just had Paul Hood, author of *Estate Planning for Modern Families*, on my radio show. He and other attorneys (and probably even some of your own acquaintances) could come up with stories of how a second spouse cut the children from the first marriage out of their parent's estate, in spite of the promises made by that parent to the children. Honestly, they may be right. I have not had that experience. In all but one of the situations in which I have been involved, the surviving spouse has honored the wishes of their deceased spouse.

I think it is up to the attorney to describe the possibilities to the client, as well as the advantages and disadvantages of different approaches and let the client decide which option makes the most sense for them. I think this idea is worth considering if there is sufficient trust, particularly in cases involving a long-term relationship when the financially stronger spouse's primary goal is to make sure that their partner/spouse has enough money to live on comfortably throughout their lifetime.

Trust Basics and Situations When a Trust May Be Appropriate

In this chapter we went straight to the fun stuff, but, before we go too much further, we had better make sure everyone understands the basics of trusts.

What is a trust? A trust is basically an agreement to have a trustee administer your assets in a way that is consistent with your wishes. Trusts can be funded either during your lifetime, or at your death. The trust agreement can be revocable, meaning that you can change it, or it can be irrevocable, meaning that you cannot change it. A testamentary trust is one that takes effect after you die. A revocable trust is a trust that is usually funded while you are alive but you can change any time you like. Basically, a testamentary trust allows you to control from the grave…sometimes not a bad idea.

As I have indicated, trusts are not always appropriate or needed. If you want to benefit your partner and your biological family, you might simply say *"X percent to one beneficiary, and X percent to another beneficiary."* If the only asset left in your estate after your death is an IRA or retirement plan, this might make perfect sense.

Other times, you may have just a small amount of money that you would like to leave to a young child. In that case, you may want to put the money into a Section 529 Plan. That way you don't have to mess around with trust fees, trustee fees, and an extra tax return. In situations where there is not that much money anyway, the Section 529 Plan may have more favorable tax implications than a trust.

Naming a Trust as the Beneficiary of an IRA

You must be very careful if you are going to name a trust as the beneficiary of your IRA. Most people do not get this right. The trust must be carefully and properly drafted. The difference between doing the trust right and doing the trust wrong can mean the difference between your beneficiary having a million dollars twenty years after your death and having nothing. Don't pay taxes now, pay taxes later. If you do it wrong, you pay taxes now. If you do it right, you're paying taxes later. If the underlying asset is an IRA or other retirement plan, a poorly drafted trust can trigger an avalanche of income taxes.

Using a Trust to Provide Protection for a Minor

The most common type of trust is a trust which is established for the benefit of a minor child. Whether it is your own child, an adopted child, a niece, or a nephew, if you are leaving an appreciable amount of money to a minor, you almost always want that money to go into a trust. Without a trust, that money gets transferred under the laws of the Uniform Gift to Minors Act. Depending on what state you live in, this means that the child will have *unlimited* access to that money at age 18 or 21. I really don't think that's a very good idea, particularly if the child is very young right now and you don't know a lot about their personality. You want to know that the child is responsible and won't go out and spend all the money right away. Some children are spendthrifts who cannot hang on to money, and need the structure of a trust well into adulthood and beyond.

The trust for a minor will protect the minor from self-inflicted bad judgment, it will protect them from creditors, and it could protect their assets in the event of a failed marriage later in life. It will even protect them from irresponsible actions by the other parent, if that is an issue. I find it interesting that, even though there can be enormous complications that develop when a minor child inherits money from a deceased parent, many parents with minor children do not feel the need to prepare wills or other documents that will protect those children.

Typically, a trust for a minor might read something like this: upon my death, my minor child receives income, plus the right to invade principal for health, maintenance, and support. So in this case, the minor child would receive the interest from the trust's assets, but can also ask the trustee for additional money to cover medical bills, housing expenses, etc. The trust then goes on to read that, at age 25, we give the child a third of the principal. At age 30, we give them another third, and at age 35, we give them the balance remaining in the account and terminate the trust. The terms can vary, depending on the child and your view of the world. Some of my clients set up trusts where their children do not get any principal until they are 50 years old.

Trusts for Adult Beneficiaries

Some adults never really develop money sense. You still want to provide for them, whether they are your own children, your nieces and nephews, or even children of your partner. You may disagree with what they are doing financially—they may be goodhearted people who, for whatever reason, cannot seem to hold down a job. Maybe money goes right through their pockets, or they get involved in a bad marriage. You want to protect these people, but if you leave them money outright, there is a very good chance that the money will disappear too quickly—and there goes the safety net that you had intended to provide them.

The solution is to provide them with a trust. A trust will protect them from themselves. It will protect them from their creditors, which can be especially significant if you leave behind a large IRA. The Supreme Court has officially ruled that *Inherited IRAs* are not considered an exempt asset in bankruptcy, so your retirement plans and IRAs can be seized by your heir's creditors if they inherit them directly. A trust will protect your heirs from their spouse, and, equally significantly, it will protect them from a *future ex-spouse*. We all know someone who has been financially devastated by a divorce. You don't want the money that you left to your adult child ending up in the hands of his or her estranged former spouse.

Giving Your Beneficiaries the Right to Disclaim[4] to Other Beneficiaries

Let's assume that you have an adult child who may eventually have his or her own children. You might want to provide your child, who is your beneficiary, with the option to "disclaim" their inheritance. Or, you could name your spouse or partner as your beneficiary, and give them the right to disclaim to your child—and then also give your child the right to disclaim to a trust for his/her child or children. By disclaiming, the first beneficiary steps aside and allows the next people in line, the second or third beneficiaries, to claim the inheritance.

For discussion's sake, let's say that you have two children, Lucy and Ricky, and they each have two children. Lucy is doing really well financially, but Ricky is just getting by and will probably need to use his inheritance. You can say, "I leave my estate to my children equally, but I'm going to give each child the right to disclaim to their own kids." After your death, Lucy says, "Hey, I'm making a lot of money and I don't really need more to live on. My parent left me a lot of money in an IRA and retirement plan, and the money will be worth more to my children than it is to me. Since I'd just leave this money to them in my own will anyway I'm going to disclaim it." And if she does this, Lucy's children will receive their grandparent's IRA and retirement plan.

On the other hand, Ricky might say, "Hey, I'd love to disclaim, but I just need the money." If he does this, then he receives his inheritance, and his children receive nothing. There is also a third option: take some and disclaim the rest. Disclaimers offer a lot of flexibility, and that makes them a great estate planning tool.

A Trust for a Special Needs Beneficiary

You may need a trust for a beneficiary with special needs. You may have someone in your life who is receiving (or potentially expecting to receive) some kind of government benefit, like Supplemental Security Income (SSI), or maybe they require specialty medications, or government housing. If you leave money outright to someone who is receiving government support, the government is entitled to take that money back and reimburse itself for the amount that they have already paid out in benefits. Receiving money outright can also cause a

---

[4] I only briefly cover disclaimers here because it isn't an issue unique to same-sex couples. For a much more thorough discussion of disclaimers see *Retire Secure!* (Wiley, 2006 and 2009) which is geared towards a more general audience.

special needs beneficiary to lose any government benefits they are currently receiving—so very careful planning is needed when a special needs beneficiary is involved. And, in case you were wondering, the government will know that the beneficiary has received the money, because the beneficiary's Social Security number must be listed on your estate tax return, and on life insurance claims forms. Typically, a special needs trust says that the trustee can pay for certain basic things the beneficiary needs, such as food, clothing and shelter, but it is worded in such a way that the government cannot appropriate the money. It would be very unlikely that the beneficiary could successfully petition the trust to receive money for a vacation. A special needs trust is an extremely important document for a limited population. If you have a special needs child, or special needs adult, and you want to provide for that person, a special needs trust is appropriate.

Choosing a Trustee for Your Trust

Who are you going to name as the trustee? This is a big question. Let's assume that you have multiple children, or multiple nieces and nephews, around age 35, and one of your beneficiaries is a spendthrift. You are afraid that one day the spendthrift child will end up living under a bridge. So, rather than leave this child money outright, you set up a trust for their benefit. Now the question is, who are you going to name as trustee? The traditional answer to that question was usually a bank. The problems with naming a bank as a trustee is that banks charge pretty high fees, and, because of the employee turnover, there may not even be anyone still working there after your death who knows what your intent was when you created the trust. There are times when you cannot avoid using a bank as trustee, but a bank is rarely my first choice.

Neither do I recommend naming an attorney as trustee. Some attorneys name themselves as trustee when they draft wills and trusts for their clients, but I believe there is an inherent conflict of interest in that scenario. Furthermore, being a trustee requires a special skill set—it requires knowing the individual very well, so that informed decisions are made with respects to their trust. Banks and attorneys usually do not know their clients that well, which is another reason why I do not like to name them as trustees. Who do I prefer to name as trustee? I usually recommend naming siblings or other family members as the trustee, not because it is the best choice, but because it is usually the best of the bad choices. It can be a very difficult role for a family member to fulfill, but at least the family member knew your wishes and your feelings, and is more likely to act in the beneficiaries' best interests.

Is Using a Trust a Good Idea for You?

Using a trust is a good idea when you want to provide for your partner or same-sex spouse for their life, and then ultimately return your wealth to your beneficiaries when your partner dies. This strategy assumes that you and your partner have different beneficiaries, so you should use it when you are not interested in providing for your partner's beneficiaries.

If your trust defines income as a percentage of principal, the income beneficiary (most likely your partner) will receive a fixed percentage of the balance of the trust. At his or her death, your end beneficiaries will receive the balance of the trust. The income beneficiary benefits when the corpus (principal) if the trust increases. And the ultimate beneficiaries benefit from the growing principal because, after the death of your surviving partner, they will get more money.

The other alternative, as discussed above, is having an oral or even written agreement with your partner about what will be in your partner's will regarding the money you leave your partner. This solution is the least costly and the least paper-work heavy, but it will only work if you have complete trust and faith that your partner will abide by your agreement after your death.

6

‖‖‖‖‖‖‖‖‖‖‖‖‖‖‖‖

The Changing World of Health Insurance

Health is a human necessity; health is a human right.

— James Lenhart, *Conversations for Paco*

Main Topics

- If I get married, will my marriage affect my eligibility for a health care tax credit?

- Can I exclude the cost of my spouse's health coverage from my gross income?

KEY IDEA

Under the Affordable Care Act (ACA), there are significant new opportunities in health care coverage and potential tax savings. You should know your new rights, but also be leery of some traps that could make getting married more expensive.

Introduction: The Affordable Care Act

The Affordable Care Act (ACA), unofficially known as "Obamacare," offers new health care insurance options for same-sex couples, as well as single gay, lesbian, bisexual, and transgender individuals. Under the ACA, the health insurance marketplaces (organizations set up in each state to create markets for buying health insurance coverage through private insurance companies) are prohibited from discriminating on the basis of sexual orientation or gender identity. The ACA also prohibits discrimination in all health plans that receive federal funding. One interesting complication of the ACA is that many companies and organizations that previously extended health insurance coverage to the same-sex *partners* of their employees are now terminating those benefits if the couple remains unmarried!

In general, though, the ACA offers welcome developments that will have enormous implications for those most in need. Of course, this health care insurance still must be purchased, but many taxpayers are eligible for reduced costs through the use of tax credits.

Filing Requirements for Tax Credits

The ACA offers a tax credit to eligible individuals to help with health care purchases that are made through the government's Health Insurance Marketplace. Advance payments of this tax credit can be sent directly to the insurer by the government; the tax credit is then applied towards the monthly insurance payments, resulting in lower monthly premiums. Individuals and married couples whose estimated incomes are less than the thresholds will be eligible for these tax credits to lower their health care premiums. To see if you are eligible for this tax credit, you should visit the following website:

www.irs.gov/uac/Am-I-eligible-to-claim-the-Premium-Tax-Credit%3F.

The income eligibility requirement means that some same-sex partners having comparable incomes will each be eligible for federal tax credits if they are unmarried, but will not be eligible for tax credits if they are legally married. The income thresholds change every year, but as an example, let's say each partner has an individual income of $45,000. If the partners remain unmarried, at that income level, they may both be eligible for individual health care tax credits. However, if they legally marry, their joint income of $90,000 may make them both ineligible for a tax credit. This is because the income threshold for married couples is not twice that of the threshold for single individuals—in fact, it's substantially less. Or, let's say one partner has an income of $90,000 and the other has an income of $20,000. The lower-earning partner will be eligible for a health care tax credit (and possibly other tax credits) if he remains single. But, if the couple gets married, their joint (combined) income will be significantly higher, and both will more than likely be ineligible for the tax credits. Even considering the loss of the health care tax credit, it may still be beneficial for the couple to marry and file a joint federal income tax return. The higher-earning partner may be in a higher tax bracket as a single filer, and may benefit from falling into a lower tax bracket by filing jointly with his spouse. The tax savings on the higher earner's wages could offset the fact that they are not eligible for health care tax credits. It's important to remember that you no longer have the option to file two single returns once you are legally married. You can either file married filing jointly or married filing separately, but filing single is no longer possible.

In addition, same-sex couples must remember that if they are legally married, the ACA requires them to file a *joint* federal income tax return to be eligible to receive tax credits to lower their health care premiums. These tax credits are not available if you are married but choose to file separately. As we frequently recommend, it is critical to run the numbers when multiple variables come into play.

New Tax Regulations for Employer Provided Health Care Plans for Same-Sex Couples

Before the Supreme Court ruling striking down part of the Defense of Marriage Act (DOMA), even if an employee's health care plan at work covered their same-sex spouse and that spouse was enrolled in the employer's health plan, the employer was required to calculate the fair market value of the spousal benefit and add that amount to the employee's federal taxable income. The employee was taxed on the value of the spousal benefit. And, in most instances, the part of the health care premium paid by the employee for his or her spouse was also taxed. The portion of the health insurance premium paid by the employer for the spousal benefit, and the portion of the health care costs that were paid by the employee for the spousal benefit were both treated as taxable income.

But the Supreme Court ruling has changed this calculation so that same-sex couples are treated the same way as straight couples. The value of the spousal benefit is no longer added to the employee's federal taxable income and, in most cases, the entire premium will not be subject to federal income tax. In addition, an employee can now make pre-tax contributions to a Section 125 Cafeteria Plan on behalf of a same-sex spouse. A cafeteria plan allows participants to receive certain benefits on a pre-tax basis. Health care costs for married same-sex couples can be paid out of pre-tax cafeteria plan dollars. The amount that the employee pays for spousal coverage is excluded from the employee's gross income and is not subject to federal income or federal employment taxes.

Before the DOMA decision, same-sex spousal benefits could not be treated on a pre-tax basis. Now, a same-sex spouse is also eligible for federally tax-free reimbursements for medical expenses from an employee spouse's Health Savings Account (HSA), Flexible Spending Account (FSA), or Health Reimbursement Arrangement (HRA). The tax savings from combinations of these provisions can easily add up to thousands of dollars. Your tax savings will vary and depend upon such factors as the cost of the health care coverage for your spouse, the medical expenses incurred by your spouse, and your current tax bracket.

We mentioned in the income tax chapter that same-sex couples who were legally married prior to the DOMA ruling but had filed their tax returns as single now have the option of filing amended tax returns for prior years. You might also be able to file an amended return to retroactively claim a credit or refund if you purchased same-sex spouse health coverage benefits or fringe benefits that were provided by your employer. These benefits were probably included in your taxable income at the time, but are now excludable from federal taxable income if you are a legally married couple.

You can also claim a refund for any relevant federal employment taxes that were paid under the old law. For example, the amount of Social Security tax and Medicare tax that was assessed on a higher wage base because health care costs for your same sex spouse were included in your wages (instead of being properly excluded from your wages) should qualify for a tax refund. Such exclusions from gross income may put you in a lower tax bracket. Note, however, that the statute of limitations for filing a refund claim is generally three years from the date the return was filed or two years from the date the tax was paid, whichever is later. Filing an amended return as a married couple is optional, and might or might not be to your advantage. Some couples might actually owe additional taxes to the IRS for previous years if they file amended returns reflecting a married status. A conversation with your tax advisor, followed by a tax assessment for "married filing jointly" versus filing as two single taxpayers would be sensible. Then, depending upon the result, either you or your CPA could file amended returns and request a refund.

A number of other protections are available to same-sex couples as well. For example, hospitals must allow visitation by a same-sex partner. Same-sex spouses must be afforded the same treatment as opposite-sex spouses for long-term care, such as nursing home care under Medicaid. Same-sex couples have the same rights as others to name a representative to make medical decisions on a patient's behalf.

The Financial Implications of Marriage on Same-Sex Health Insurance Options

Please, don't jump to the conclusion that getting married will save taxes on health care premiums in all situations. There are negative financial implications as well, and it comes back to running the numbers. For instance, our firm has at least one client who is choosing not to get married now because the financially dependent partner (the partner with a much smaller income) can get inexpensive health insurance through the ACA. The couple would lose that inexpensive health care option if they got married because their joint income would make them ineligible for the tax credits. The financially independent partner has health care through her employer—but the company she works for does not offer health care benefits for unmarried same-sex couples.

For this couple, between the marriage income tax penalty (see Chapter 4) and the additional cost of the higher health care premium, there are substantial financial advantages to remaining unmarried—at least for the time being. Their plan is to wait until the financially dependent partner qualifies for Medicare, and then get married. That strategy might work out well. On the other hand, it could be a disastrous tax decision if the financially stronger partner dies before they get married. For instance, the surviving partner would have to pay the income taxes on her *Inherited IRA* and those taxes could far exceed the health care premium savings. The dependent partner would also lose out on the option to collect the spouse's Social Security benefits. It might be a "penny wise and pound" foolish strategy.

Deciding if it makes financial sense to get married is sometimes clear-cut, but sometimes not. You have to weigh the objective advantages and disadvantages; then, at least, you will know where you stand. What we are trying to do with this book is point out some of the objective criteria so that you can make informed financial decisions.

7

‖‖‖‖‖‖‖‖‖‖‖‖‖‖‖‖

Federal and State Gift, Estate and Inheritance Taxes

To tax and to please, no more than to love and be wise, is not given to men.

— Edmund Burke

Main Topics

- Defining transfer taxes

- Contrasting the impact of transfer taxes for married *vs.* unmarried beneficiaries

- Gifting as a way to reduce death taxes

KEY IDEA

Reducing estate and inheritance taxes provides another financial incentive to get married.

An Overview of Transfer Taxes

The federal gift and estate tax is a transfer tax levied when individuals transfer assets to others during their lifetime or at their death. It is rare that individuals pay gift taxes during their lifetime. Therefore, it is much more common for the transfer tax to be imposed on the transfer of assets at their death. This is also true of state transfer taxes.

Assets that you transfer to a spouse either at death or while you are alive are treated much more favorably that assets transferred to a non-spouse (partner). If married, you are allowed to transfer an unlimited amount of property to your U.S. citizen spouse, during your lifetime or at your death, free of transfer taxes. This is called the Unlimited Marital Deduction.

The transfer taxes imposed by states, often called inheritance taxes, vary widely from state to state, but always are more favorable for spouses leaving money to spouses than individuals leaving or gifting money to non-spouses (partners).

For federal transfer or estate tax purposes, it may not make any difference whether you get married or not depending on the size of your estate. With respect to transfers to non-spouse beneficiaries, the IRS sets the upper limit on how much money individuals are allowed to transfer to others each year and during their lifetime before they incur a transfer tax. In 2015, you are allowed to give gifts of up to $14,000 each year ($28,000 if married) to one individual and a total of $5.43 million over your lifetime or at your death. If you gift more than $14,000 per beneficiary ($28,000 if married), you are supposed to file a gift tax return, and the excess gift reduces the amount of your estate that can pass transfer tax-free at your death.

Every year most individuals routinely file a Form 1040 income tax return. But that tax return is based only on your income, not on the transfer of any assets you may have received or given. Transfer taxes are a separate beast, and should be treated and thought of differently than income taxes. For state purposes, an inheritance tax is calculated separately for each heir based on what they receive and how the beneficiary is related to the deceased person. Depending on the relationship, each beneficiary might be taxed at a different rate. For federal purposes, an estate tax is imposed on the entire value of the estate of the deceased person, but it is still necessary to consider the relationship of the beneficiary to the deceased. For the vast majority of our readers, income taxes will be far more of a concern than transfer taxes, but we need to cover transfer taxes for completeness. And if transfer taxes are a concern in your own situation you need to know that there are new opportunities for reducing them in light of the DOMA decision and its aftermath.

With the unlimited marital deduction now available to same-sex couples that get married, you could give or leave your spouse a billion dollars, and there would not be one cent of federal gift or estate tax. The transfer taxes charged by individual states are so disparate that a discussion of them is beyond the scope of this book but, in general, a spouse is treated much more favorably by the states than a partner who receives a gift or inheritance. In my own state of Pennsylvania, there is no inheritance tax charged on transfers to your surviving spouse. There is, however, a 4.5% tax on transfers to your children, a 12% tax on transfers to your siblings, and a 15% tax on transfers to any other heir.

So, let's assume you have a $1 million estate you intend to leave to your partner. Obviously, there will be no federal estate tax. If you die in Pennsylvania without getting married, your partner will have a $150,000 tax. If you do get married, there will be no tax for your spouse.

Getting Married to Save Taxes at the Second Death

Suppose, though, that your partner has a significant amount of wealth ($5 million) in her own right. You die first, leaving her $2 million. A month later, your partner dies suddenly and your heirs stand to inherit $7 million. Since your partner's exemption amount is only $5,430,000, her death is a tax nightmare for the heirs. If you marry, it doesn't have to be. The American Taxpayer Relief Act of 2012 introduced a wonderful concept called portability. Portability refers to the provision that any exemption amount that is left over after the first death is automatically added to the exemption amount of the surviving spouse provided that a federal estate tax return is filed at the time of the first spouse's death. Only $2 million of your $5.43 million exemption amount would have been used at the time of your death. And if you were legally married, your unused exemption amount of $3.43 million ($5.43 million - $2 million) would be added to your spouse's own exemption of $5.43 million. Your surviving spouse now has an exemption amount of $8.86 million. And even though she died with an estate worth $7 million, your heirs would not have to pay federal estate tax. The portability rules do not apply to unmarried partners, so this is one example of how marriage can be financially beneficial for some couples.

Gifting Can Eliminate Inheritance Taxes

Most people don't like to give away their money or their property, even to their spouse, to reduce taxes at their death. But some gifting may be appropriate in certain situations. There is no federal gift tax imposed on married couples gifting money to one another. If you have complete faith that you and your partner will stay together, and you think you may die within a few years, you might consider gifts to reduce state inheritance taxes. For example, in Pennsylvania, transfers from one person to another that are made more than one year prior to death will escape the 15% state inheritance tax applicable on transfers to *non-relatives*. Accordingly, it is possible under specific circumstances that gifting between partners in same-sex marriages can reduce the assessment of the Pennsylvania inheritance tax.

While gifting is a good planning option for many same-sex married couples, you must pay attention to the gift tax and death tax laws of your own state. Although Pennsylvania allows transfers made more than one year prior to death to escape the inheritance tax, in other states only transfers made more than two or three years prior to death will escape taxation. As always, please see your tax advisor or a local attorney regarding the laws in your state.

Additional Gift Considerations

If you have assets that are highly appreciated, such as stock, you may want to leave them to your spouse as part of an inheritance rather than as a gift. If your spouse receives a highly appreciated asset as part of an inheritance, the value is "stepped up." So, if your spouse has to sell the asset, her capital gain will be calculated based on the asset's value at the time she inherits it from you. If the stock is given as a gift, there is a loss of this "step-up in basis." Finally, it may be advisable to consider transferring assets into a jointly held account to reduce inheritance taxes by half.

I must stress that a gifting strategy is a sensible option for relatively few couples. The older, richer, and sicker you are, the more appropriate it is to consider gifting. Gifting can work for same-sex couples who live in a state that does not have a gift tax but does have an inheritance or estate tax. However, you must trust your spouse beyond a shadow of a doubt if you are going to gift away part of your money or other property. Furthermore, you must know how many years prior to death that transfers will escape your state's inheritance or estate tax. Using careful tax planning with a knowledgeable advisor or local attorney in your state, this strategy can work for some same-sex couples. Many states have their own inheritance or estate tax rules in place regarding transfers in contemplation of death, so working with a professional who knows the law in your state is a good idea. In most cases, however, getting married will be the best gift and estate tax reduction action you could take.

8

||||||||||||||||||||

Putting All the
Pieces Together:
A Case Study

The whole is greater than the sum of its parts.

— Aristotle

Main Topics

- Extensive case study using multiple strategies

- Recommendations for further reading

- Synergy between timing Social Security benefits and Roth IRA conversions

- Life altering variations for Dr. Dan, Baker Bob, and Penniless Perry

> ## KEY IDEA
>
> No *one* key unlocks the treasure of financial security
> and getting the most out of what you've got; the solution
> is more like a combination lock where you have to get
> a number of things right to maximize your assets and
> financial security.

Introduction to How the We Put the Pieces Together

In Chapter 2, I demonstrated the difference between inheriting an IRA from a non-married partner as opposed to a spouse, and showed that the tax benefits of being married can be enormous if you inherit an IRA or retirement plan from your spouse. In one example from Chapter 2, the survivor was better off by $700,000, with the only difference being he married his partner before his partner died. The entire difference was attributed to the different tax treatment of the IRA at the death of the IRA owner, who, in our example, was the first to die.

In Chapter 3, I demonstrated the potential increase in Social Security benefits that a married couple can receive, especially if they use the *Apply and Suspend* strategy. The difference there amounted to an additional $1,500,000 for the surviving spouse—there are no Social Security spousal benefits if you are not married.

Now we are going to present a comprehensive picture of the benefits of combining the individual strategies; offering the combination number to the lock, so to speak.

The basic steps:

1. Get married and name *your spouse*, not *your partner*, as the beneficiary of your IRAs and retirement plans (Chapter 2).

2. Take advantage of the spousal benefits for Social Security, and use *Apply and Suspend* if appropriate (Chapter 3).

3. Do a series of Roth IRA conversions over a number of years, preferably during low income years that are typically between the year you retire and the year you turn age 70½ (when you have to start taking

required minimum distributions (RMD) from your traditional IRA and/or retirement plan).

The rest of the chapter will be a detailed case study that proves our assertion that in at least situations close to Doctor Dan and Baker Bob, there are enormous financial benefits to be gained from getting married. If you want to skip the details of this is chapter, please skip to "Final Note," on page 117.

I wrestled with the question of whether to include our Roth IRA conversion analysis in this book because I think it is such a crucial element of planning for most IRA and retirement plan owners. The reason we didn't include an in-depth analysis of the subject in this book is that Roth IRA conversions are not really an issue specific to same-sex couples—and furthermore, the topic is very complicated. I wrote an entire book devoted to just that subject, *The Roth Revolution – Pay Taxes Once and Never Again* (Morgan James, 2011). That said, I believe all IRA owners should at least consider whether a Roth IRA conversion is appropriate. If it is appropriate, then the next question is when, and how much. So, for our "putting all the pieces together" conclusion, we include the ideal timing and amounts for Doctor Dan's Roth IRA conversions, without devoting a chapter specifically to Roth IRA conversions.

Another excellent resource for Roth IRA conversions as well as most IRA and retirement and estate planning information is the third edition (2015) of my flagship book, *Retire Secure, Getting the Most out of What You've Got*.

The "running the numbers" process we used to arrive at our ideal timing and amount of Roth IRA conversions is described in the appendix.

Therefore, I ask you to take it on faith that I have done the research and analysis to arrive at my Roth IRA conversion numbers for our case study.

And in case you are wondering if I am qualified to make these determinations, please know that, in 1998, I wrote and published the very first peer reviewed Roth IRA conversion article. It tied for "Best Article of the Year" in the tax journal published by the American Institute of CPAs, *The Tax Adviser*.[1] So you could say that I am the one of the pioneers of this strategy. Both my dedicated Roth IRA book and general retirement and estate planning book, *Retire Secure!* received glowing testimonials from the nation's top IRA experts. In short, the same methodology and reasoning that survived that peer review

---

[1] "IRAs After the TRA' 97 What Hath Congress Roth?" American Institute of Certified Public Accountants' *The Tax Adviser*, May 1998.

process in 1998 went into the Roth IRA conversion optimization calculations that I have used here.

Let's go back to our combination lock analogy. Although there is a benefit to analyzing Social Security and Roth IRA conversion strategies independently, we believe there is a synergy between Social Security and Roth IRA conversions. Maximizing Social Security benefits and Roth IRA conversion are not two independent processes, but rather two synergistic calculations. And what I am going to illustrate below is the synthesis of my research.

In the following graph, we compare the same two couples with identical finances, but different strategies.

The first couple

1. doesn't get married

2. both partners take Social Security at age 62

3. neither partner makes Roth IRA conversions

The second couple

1. does get married

2. uses the *Apply and Suspend* strategy at age 66 for Social Security

3. makes a series of Roth IRA conversions optimized per above discussion

Figure 8.1
Unmarried vs. Married: Net Assets Available for Retirement Years

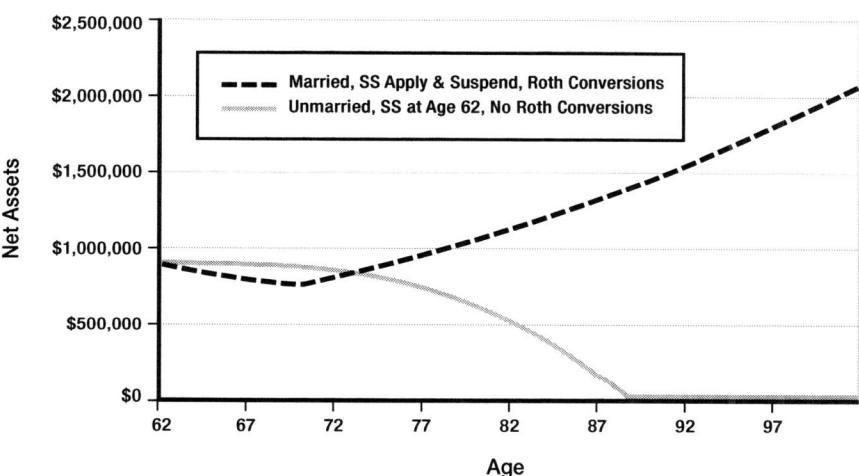

A Case Study Spanning the Later Years of Life for a Same-Sex Couple

Let's go back to the couple we've been discussing throughout these chapters, Doctor Dan and Baker Bob. For this example, both men are age 62 when Doctor Dan decides to retire. For income during his retirement, Doctor Dan has his Social Security benefits, a traditional IRA with a balance of $700,000, and after-tax savings account worth $350,000. Baker Bob has a small savings account with a balance of $50,000.[2] The men estimate that their annual living

---

[2] For our math wizards reading this, you already may be adding the numbers in your head: $700,000 + $350,000 + $50,000 = $1,100,000 in total retirement savings. Why does our graph start at a beginning value lower than $1,100,000 you might ask? We are measuring in purchasing power, not total dollars. The IRA balances must be reduced by the income tax liability that would follow if the IRA was distributed. Our couple must pay income tax on any funds withdrawn from the IRA account. For the purpose of this example, we have assumed that the income tax rate on those withdrawals to be 28%. This reduces the available assets in the IRA from $700,000 to $504,000. It is not that they are withdrawing the money from the IRA and paying all of the taxes. Subtracting the taxes is just a way of showing the purchasing power of the money in the IRA. Now take the $504,000 + $350,000 + $50,000 = $904,000. That's where our graph begins. During the course of Doctor Dan's career he saved an additional $350,000 which is held in a traditional brokerage account. The money invested in this account was already after-tax money. As with most brokerage accounts, he has earned interest and dividend income on that account, and paid any related income taxes throughout the years. Therefore, there was no need for us to make an income tax allowance for those funds or for the cash sitting in Baker Bob's savings account. We are not factoring the capital gains tax that could be substantial if the assets are highly appreciated stocks.

expenses are $75,000. Doctor Dan pays a substantial portion of those expenses, $70,000 and Baker Bob pays the balance of $5,000

Until retiring at the age of 62, Doctor Dan earned a reasonable living. His earnings record is high enough that, once retired, he is able to collect the maximum Social Security benefit possible for someone who is 62. If he chooses to take his benefits at age 62, though, he will receive 25% less (approximately $23,422) than if he waited until he was his full retirement age of 66 (approximately $31,232). Now suppose that he and Baker Bob follow my recommendation to get married, and they use the *Apply and Suspend* strategy for Doctor Dan's Social Security. Doctor Dan would apply for benefits at age 66, and then "suspend" collecting until age 70. When he finally begins to collect, he would earn an extra 8% in Delayed Retirement Credits each year, make the amount he receives *each year* approximately $41,266.

Baker Bob has held down a few part-time jobs over the years, but he is primarily responsible for their home life. Assuming he does not marry, Baker Bob, at age 62, will be able to collect only *$5,000* each year in Social Security benefits, based on his earnings record. Now let's look at what happens if he and Doctor Dan marry and Doctor Dan uses the *Apply and Suspend* technique. If Baker Bob waits till age 66 to apply, he will be able to collect a spousal Social Security benefit of $15,616 (one half of what we are estimating that Doctor Dan could collect at age 66) plus COLAs. Keep in mind that Baker Bob is not eligible to receive a spousal benefit unless they are in a *legally recognized* marriage.

Finances for this Couple While They are Both Living—Using All of the Advice in this Book

Now that we've gotten all of the details out of the way, let's review the results of the graph above. You can see that, from ages 62 to 70, if the men are married and they take our other advice, their assets decrease more rapidly than if they had remained unmarried and begun taking Social Security. There are two reasons for this, and the first should be obvious. Doctor Dan retired at age 62 and his income plummeted to zero. The second reason is that they have deliberately chosen to not collect Social Security benefits for the years they are ages 62 to 66—instead, they're going to withdraw some money from Doctor Dan's after-tax brokerage account to live on. Doctor Dan takes my advice, and applies for and suspends his Social Security benefits at age 66, while still allowing Baker Bob to collect his spousal benefits from the ages of 66 to 70. Doctor Dan waits until age 70, and then takes his full increased amount of Social Security. By delaying until age 70, he reaps the additional benefit of the 8% increases per year (plus COLAs) that has been accruing since he was age 66. As demonstrated in Chapter 3, there would have been significant benefits even if he had only held off collecting his Social Security until age 66, but holding off until age 70 is the optimal choice for him. Baker Bob's ability to collect a spousal benefit at age 66 that is based on Doctor Dan's higher earnings record, and Doctor Dan's ability to collect full Social Security benefits at age 70 rapidly makes up for the decrease in assets experienced in the early years. After only 10 years, the benefits of this approach far exceed the other alternative.

In order to strengthen their overall financial position, Dan made a series of Roth IRA conversions between age 62 and age 70. With our guidance, Dan converted the maximum amount he was able to receive as "income," without pushing the couple into a higher income tax bracket.

This brings us to one of the reasons that you have to look at these issues synergistically. A side benefit to Doctor Dan's Roth IRA conversions is that they lower Doctor Dan's RMD (required minimum distribution) from his traditional IRA, because the amount of money in the traditional IRA is reduced. A further benefit of the Roth conversion strategy is that the lower RMD at age 70 and beyond cut Doctor Dan's income taxes when he is in his highest income tax bracket. If Doctor Dan needs to withdraw money from the Roth IRA, he can do so without worrying about income tax implications. If he doesn't withdraw anything from the Roth IRA, Doctor Dan, Baker Bob, and Penniless Perry will all benefit from the income-tax free growth on the account.

We can now understand that the decrease in assets for the married couple in our graph is caused by them holding off on Social Security and paying some taxes upfront on the Roth IRA conversions.

The chart takes a significant bend upwards meaning the real benefits of our strategies start increasing dramatically when both men reach the age of 70. Baker Bob continues to collect Social Security benefits based on the spousal benefit of Doctor Dan's earnings, but now Doctor Dan also begins collecting benefits at the increased rate we discussed previously. At age 70½, Doctor Dan must begin taking RMDs from what remains of his traditional IRA. Since the balance of his traditional IRA account has been decreased by the Roth conversions done prior to age 70, the amount of his required RMD is reduced. This in turn reduces the amount of income tax payments due. Doctor Dan's initial RMD starts around $35,000. Add to that both men's Social Security benefits of $41,226 and $15,616. These three items alone total $91,842, which is more than enough income to cover their annual living expense of $75,000. (Keep in mind that all of these numbers are based on today's dollars, and would be increased for COLAs. The graph takes those adjustments into account.) Since 100% of their living expenses are met, the balance of savings in both IRA accounts and eventually the excess of the MRD over living expenses that is reinvested continues to grow throughout their lives.

Now let's take a look at the other scenario on the graph, where the men remain unmarried. Doctor Dan retires at 62, both men begin to collect Social Security benefits immediately based on their individual earnings record, and they make no Roth IRA conversions. At first, their combined Social Security benefits of $28,422 ($23,422 plus $5,000) help to cover a portion of the cost of their annual living expenses of $75,000, but they must still withdraw funds from their after-tax savings account to meet their budget requirements. (Once again, keep in mind that all of these numbers are based on today's dollars and would be increased for COLAs. The graph takes those adjustments into account.) Neither "single" man has to make any income tax payments from the ages of 62 to 69, which also helps to minimize declining assets. However, at age 70, we can see the "unmarried" line on the graph begin dropping at a more rapid pace. This is created by the income tax payments due on the higher RMDs that Doctor Dan must take starting at age 70½.

Had he transferred funds from his traditional IRA into a Roth IRA in those early years of retirement, his RMDs would have been reduced which, in turn, would have reduced his income tax payments. In addition, the only increase in Social Security benefits either of these men will see results from the annual cost of living adjustments. From the very beginning of their retirement, the unmarried couple must use a portion of their after-tax savings in order to cover their annual living expenses. By the age of 90, the men will have completely wiped out their after-tax savings and their IRA, and will have nothing but their reduced Social Security benefits as a means for financial support. If Doctor Dan dies first, his Social Security benefits will cease, and Baker Bob will spend the rest of his life living well below the federal poverty level.

On the other hand, if they take my advice to 1. get married, 2. Apply and Suspend Social Security at age 66 and take spousal benefits for Baker Bob, and 3. do Roth IRA conversions from age 62 to age 67, their spendable assets will continue to increase. At age 70, the men would have an additional $125,000 in spendable assets. At age 80, their assets grow to $406,000 and, at age 90, they'll have $1,427,000. If one of them lives beyond age 90, there would be an even greater difference. And it doesn't matter at which age they die—they would still be able to leave a healthy nest egg for Baker Bob's son, Penniless Perry.

Which of these scenarios would you rather see happen for you and your own partner?

Let's Take Our Case Study to the Next Phase in Life— The Death of One Spouse/Partner

We know that Doctor Dan is self-sufficient. If he takes my advice and invests responsibly, presumably using a well-diversified set of low cost index funds, he will be able to support himself and Baker Bob for as long as he lives. Unfortunately, we also know that Baker Bob has limited funds, and his own earnings record entitles him to a meager Social Security benefit. Baker Bob will not be able to support himself if something happens to Doctor Dan and he has to rely on his own resources. Even though Doctor Dan plans to leave all his assets to Baker Bob, he is still worried about his partner and wants to take all the appropriate steps to maximize Baker Bob's financial security if he predeceases him.

Although this should not come as a shock, the advice we gave Doctor Dan and Baker Bob while they are both alive will make an even bigger difference to Baker Bob if Doctor Dan predeceases him. Refer to "A Case Study Spanning the Later Years of Life for a Same-Sex Couple" (above) to see the specifics of our partners prior to Doctor Dan's death.

Figure 8.2 on the following page displays the three possible scenarios: (1) married with the couple having followed all my strategic advice; (2) remaining unmarried and not following any of my advice (under existing laws related to *Inherited IRAs*); and (3) the unmarried scenario using the likely future laws governing *Inherited IRAs* (a total of five years to distribute the *Inherited IRA*).

Finances for the Surviving Partner/Spouse—Using All of the Advice in this Book

Let's run the numbers again comparing "taking my advice" and "not taking my advice." This time we are assuming that one partner dies. We will compare the same benefits that we discussed in the previous scenarios: getting married versus remaining unmarried and the effects on the IRA; *Applying and Suspending* at age 66 versus taking Social Security at age 62; and rolling a portion of the traditional IRA into a Roth IRA during the transitional years between age 62 and 70 versus keeping all money in the traditional IRA. Keep in mind that all of our current scenarios are a direct continuation of our previous scenarios. Previously we tracked the growth or loss of the couple's assets assuming the men lived beyond 100 years. For this scenario we are simply taking the previous accounts to the end of their 78th year, when Doctor Dan dies. All balances at that point are going to be inherited by Baker Bob.

Figure 8.2

Following vs. Ignoring the Advice in this Book:
Assets for Dependent Spouse/Partner After Death of Higher Wage Earner

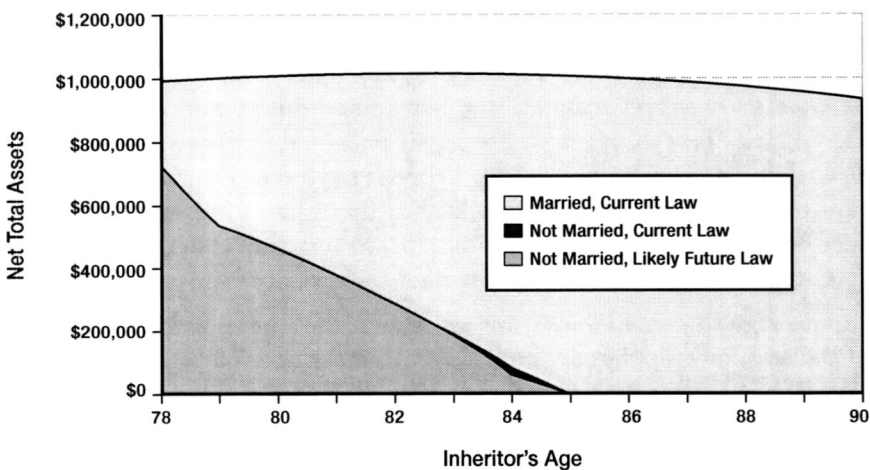

Assumptions for this graph (at the time of Doctor Dan's death) are listed below.[3]

---

[3] 1. Baker Bob held a few part time jobs over the years, but is unemployed at the age of 60. He has $107,748 of his own savings in after-tax assets.

2. If married, and using our strategies, Baker Bob inherits a traditional IRA from Doctor Dan worth $535,997 and a Roth IRA worth $603,405 (before tax implications).

3. If unmarried, and not using our strategies, Baker Bob inherits a traditional IRA worth $857,750 (before tax implications).

4. For the single scenarios, assets are decreased in the first year for Pennsylvania inheritance tax under current law. Baker Bob elects to collect Social Security of $5,000 (plus COLAs) at age 62 if unmarried in the less favorable scenario, or $15,616 (plus COLAs) as a spousal benefit at age 66 if he and Doctor Dan were married and he's able to collect on Doctor Dan's earnings history.

5. During his life time, married Doctor Dan applied and suspended his Social Security Benefits at age 66.

6. Annual living expenses, $75,000 (plus COLAs for inflation)

7. Includes a 3% Rate of Inflation and 6% Rate of Return

8. Balances shown include a 28% Federal Tax Allowance on traditional Retirement Account Balances.

9. We are measuring IRAs net of taxes. That means we are valuing a $1,000,000 IRA at $720,000 which is calculated by multiplying the IRA value times 28% tax rate (or $280,000), and subtracting the tax from the value of the account. This gives us the purchasing power of the IRA and allows us to add it to the after tax investments and the Roth IRA for a net total.

The top line in Figure 8.2 represents the married and widowed Baker Bob. At the age of 79 he receives an inheritance from his husband, Doctor Dan of $1,139,402 (unadjusted for income tax). The inheritance consists of a Roth IRA totaling $603,405 and a traditional IRA of $535,997.[4]

After the first year in the "Married Current Law" scenario we can see that the couple's wealth doesn't change significantly. This is a result of the married couple taking advantage of all the advice I suggested for the years between age 62 and the year Doctor Dan passed away. This provided Baker Bob with over $300,000 more in spendable assets *from the very first day of his inheritance*, as compared to the unmarried scenario. And that is only the first of several advantages from which Baker Bob will benefit, simply because the couple married. Baker Bob will also receive:

1. higher Social Security benefits based on his spouse's benefits after Doctor Dan *Applied and Suspended* his benefits at 66 (or approximately $41,226 plus COLAs)

2. the advantage of the tax free Roth IRA distributions

3. the advantage of the RMD rules for rolling over a spousal IRA. (As we saw in Chapter 2 this benefit alone, in contrast to the draconian rules for a non-spouse beneficiary might be enough to justify marriage.)

Between the ages of 62 to 67, Doctor Dan rolled a significant amount of money from his traditional IRA into a Roth IRA. This means that Doctor Dan paid the income tax up front on those rollovers, which in turn reduced the balance of the traditional IRA and the amount of inheritance tax Baker Bob had to pay on it when he died. It also allows the $603,405 balance in the *Inherited Roth IRA* to grow tax free, and to be withdrawn tax free. And because the couple married, Baker Bob is able to roll Dr. Dan's IRA into his own IRA, which will allow for lower RMDs and lower income tax payments.[5] Ultimately,

---

[4] Again for our math wizards: yes, Baker Bob inherited $1,139,402. So why does our graph start below $1,000.000? Let me explain. We start our calculation with Baker Bob's inheritance excluding any income tax implications. We must do this because we have to calculate the Inheritance Tax on the entire balance of the inheritance. But for the balances carried forward on our graph, we want to reduce the traditional IRA by the 28% income tax assumption to calculate its actual purchasing power. So our beginning balance is calculated as follows: Roth $603,405 + (Traditional IRA $535,997 – $150,079 [28% tax]) = $989,323. This is the starting point of our graph.

[5] Based on the Uniform Life Table IRS Publication 590.

if the couple marries, Baker Bob will have more than enough assets to support himself to the end of his life. If he dies at age 90, Baker Bob will still have spendable assets of $938,202 that he can leave to his heirs.

Now let's look at Baker Bob's inheritance, assuming that the couple ignored all of my advice and did *not* get married prior to Doctor Dan's death. Carried forward from our previous unmarried partners, Baker Bob's $50,000 savings account has now grown to $107,748. This is his own money, so there are no tax implications on the account when Doctor Dan dies.

As an unmarried man, Doctor Dan had a traditional IRA with a balance of $857,750 when he passed away. Baker Bob must pay Pennsylvania inheritance tax on that entire amount. The 15% tax, or $128,663, totally wipes out his personal savings account balance. So again we start our graph with the tax adjusted *Inherited IRA* balance of $617,580 ($857,750 less 28% Federal Income Tax to give us the purchasing power of the IRA), and add Bob's own money of $107,748—for a total $725,328. And here we see a significant decrease in assets the very first year of our analysis. This decrease is caused by the large state inheritance tax payment due the first year after Doctor Dan's death.

Even after the first year, we continue to see a rather steep reduction in assets every year thereafter. Another downside to not getting married is that Baker Bob can only collect the $5,000 (plus COLAs) in Social Security benefits that he had been receiving since turning 62. This is not nearly enough to cover his cost of living of $75,000 annually (plus COLAs). Not only must he withdraw money from his *Inherited IRA* to cover living expenses, he must also withdraw enough money to cover the income tax payments due on these withdrawals. Because of Baker Bob's shortage of assets, his distributions must be larger than the RMD under the "Not Married, Current Law" scenario. This causes him to run out of assets within seven years of Doctor Dan's death, preventing him from taking full advantage of the *stretch IRA* (and more importantly, from eating).

Now let's look at what will happen to the unmarried survivor, if the law is changed as we expect it to be. Baker Bob must take enough in distributions to fully deplete the *Inherited IRA* within five years. We recommended that he spread out these distributions as evenly as possible, in an effort to minimize the impact of the income tax due on the distributions. Unfortunately, Baker Bob runs out of assets during the seventh year after Doctor Dan's death. There is not a significant difference in asset growth/depletion between the two unmarried scenarios, because in the example under the current law, Bob spent more than the RMD and depleted the IRA in seven years—similar spending to this five year example. However, we chose to include both unmarried options in our graph just to maintain consistency. In both unmarried scenarios, Baker Bob runs out of money at the age of 85.

So once again, we see the significance of the couple marrying. If the couple marries, Doctor Dan can be assured that there will be enough spendable assets to cover Baker Bob's expenses through the end of his life. If the couple doesn't marry, given these assumptions, Baker Bob will run out of money at the age of 85. Let's break down these differences.

The *very first day* that Baker Bob inherits the assets of husband Doctor Dan, he will have $300,000 more, simply because the couple married. In addition, out of the total inheritance from his spouse, Baker Bob would have received $603,405 in a Roth IRA. Baker Bob should spend any funds from the Traditional IRA first, which allows the Roth IRA to continue to grow income tax free. Keep in mind that, when the time comes that Baker Bob needs to withdraw funds from the Roth IRA, all distributions, including the growth on the account, will be 100% income tax free.

The first year after Doctor Dan's death would be the only year in which married Baker Bob must withdraw more funds from his inheritance than he would have to if he were unmarried. First, because he inherited $300,000 more as a married man, he must also pay more Pennsylvania inheritance tax. If he were married, his total inheritance tax bill would be $170,910 ($1,139,402 x 15%). If he were unmarried, his Pennsylvania inheritance tax bill would be $128,663 ($857,750 x 15%). Not only would his inheritance tax be less as an unmarried person, keep in mind that he also has $107,748 in his own after tax savings account to cover a large portion of the tax bill. His total IRA distributions during the first year after Doctor Dan's death would have to be $204,684 ($75,000 Living Expenses + $170,910 Inheritance Tax - $41,226 Social Security Income) if he were married, but only $90,915 ($75,000 Living Expenses + $20,915 Inheritance Tax - $5,000 Social Security Income) if he were unmarried. But even after paying more in taxes, married Baker Bob still has a larger pile of money than unmarried Baker Bob.

The second year after Doctor Dan's death, Baker Bob would be required to pay federal income taxes on the large distributions that he took the first year. If he was married, the income taxes for year two would be approximately

$48,000, and if unmarried, $20,000. As a result, year two's distributions would be $81,774 if married ($75,000 Living Expenses + $48,000 Income Tax - $41,226 Social Security Income), and if unmarried, $90,000 ($75,000 Living Expenses + $20,000 Income Tax - $5,000 Social Security Income).

Once the tax implications of the original distributions have been paid, Baker Bob's annual distributions become more reasonable. If Baker Bob were married, he would only need to take distributions of $33,774 plus income taxes due, for the remainder of his life ($75,000 living expenses - $41,226 in Social Security Income). This means that his rolled over traditional IRA would be depleted within five years, and he would only owe tax on an additional three years of distributions. After the traditional IRA is depleted in year five, he would have to begin withdrawing funds from his inherited Roth IRA. The distributions from the Roth IRA are 100% income tax free to Baker Bob.

If Baker Bob remained unmarried, his distributions from the traditional IRA would need to be much larger. This is because, as an unmarried person, Baker Bob would be receiving only $5,000 per year in Social Security benefits and all other money necessary for his financial survival would come from his inheritance. So, not only does he have to take larger distributions, but all those distributions are coming from an Inherited IRA—which means that the distributions are 100% taxable. His annual distributions would need to be around $85,000 a year ($75,000 living expenses + $15,000 income taxes - $5,000 Social Security Income). At this rate in either unmarried scenario, Baker Bob would run out of all assets before his eighty-sixth birthday.

We assume that Baker Bob will live to the age of 90. Think of the stress that he and Penniless Perry will endure trying to finance those last four years, since Baker Bob and Doctor Dan never married. If they had married, Baker Bob would never have had to worry about being a burden to his son. And what a wonderful legacy the couple could leave to Baker Bob's son—a tax free Roth IRA worth $960,213.

The Case Study Continues With the Second Death— What About the Next Generation?

It is clear that, if Baker Bob and Doctor Dan plan according to our strategies, there will be assets remaining even after Baker Bob has died. So if we now bring Penniless Perry into the picture, we can see how the differences between using our strategies and maintaining the status quo will affect the next generation.

Let's Take a Look at the Long Term Growth Potential for the Couple's Heir if They Follow All of the Advice in This Book

Penniless Perry is the beloved underemployed adopted son of Baker Bob. He was 60 when his father, Bob, passed away just before his ninety-first birthday. Although he earned about $60,000 per year, Penniless routinely spent almost every penny that he earned. Saving and preparing for retirement was never a high priority. He never thought about what would happen to him if he retired or lost his income. Prior to his father passing away, Penniless Perry's entire life savings consisted of $10,500 in a local bank account.

If you recall from the previous graph, in both of the examples where Baker Bob and Doctor Dan did not marry, there are no assets left for Penniless Perry to inherit by the time Baker Bob dies. Penniless will have to continue to work the rest of his life to support his $1,000/week lifestyle, since his Social Security income will be insufficient. And who knows what will happen if he is unable to work in his later years?

But married Doctor Dan and Baker Bob were thinking ahead to safeguard Penniless Perry's financial security. Let's assume that Baker Bob needed to spend a few years in a nursing home before he died, and that he needed to spend part of Doctor Dan's IRA on his own care. When he died, though, Bob left the balance of the assets that he had inherited from Doctor Dan, to Penniless Perry. After taxes, Perry was the proud owner of an *Inherited Roth IRA* worth $578,548. Penniless Perry thought it was criminal that he had to spend more than his life savings to pay Pennsylvania inheritance tax of 4.5% (note: children get a break on inheritance tax in Pennsylvania), which amounted to $26,035.

The inheritance and the process of dealing with his father's death was a wakeup call for Penniless Perry. After getting some reasonable retirement planning advice, he learned that if he continues to responsibly invest the Roth IRA in a well-diversified set of index funds, he may be able to retire securely if he continues to work through the age of 69. At age 70 he can retire and stop working completely, and then be able to collect $20,000 (plus COLAs) in Social Security benefits from age 70 forward.

Let's take a look at the graph of Penniless Perry's inheritance on the next page. In Figure 8.3, we see the addition of his father's Roth IRA of about $590,000. Notice how his earnings remain stagnant the first year. This is consistent with prior scenarios, where the state inheritance tax is due the year

Figure 8.3
Adult Child Inherits Assets from Widowed Parent

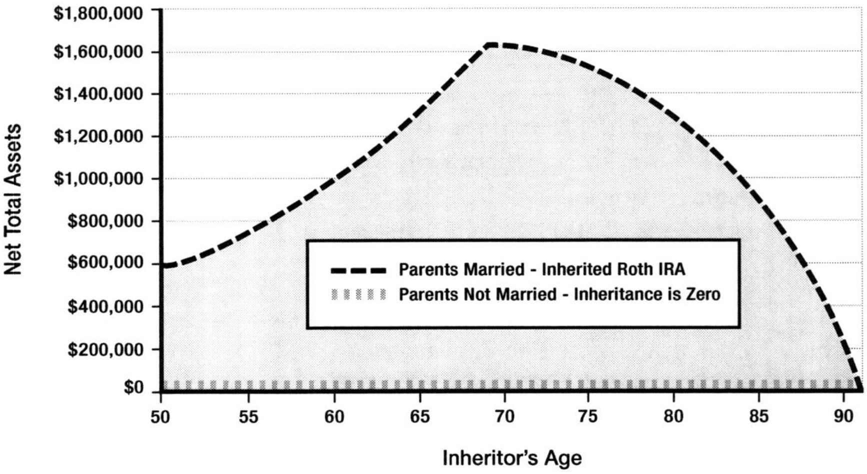

Net Total Assets (y-axis)
Inheritor's Age (x-axis)

Legend:
- - - Parents Married - Inherited Roth IRA
▮▮▮▮ Parents Not Married - Inheritance is Zero

Assumptions for this graph are listed in the footnote below.[6]

following an inheritance. In the state of Pennsylvania, the Inheritance Tax Rate for a child of the decedent is 4½%. After the first year, Penniless's inherited assets continue to grow until he retires at age 70. Although he is required to take distributions from his Inherited Roth IRA, he invests the proceeds in an after-tax account and grows that for his retirement years as well.

Once he retires, his annual living expenses exceed his Social Security income, resulting in a rapid decline of his savings. Keep in mind that the only reason this inheritance exists is because Doctor Dan and Baker Bob took my retirement and estate planning advice. Otherwise, there would have been nothing for Penniless Perry to inherit. By the time Penniless Perry retires at age 70, his savings have grown by over a million dollars. This gives him enough funds so that he can retire and live the lifestyle to which he has become accustomed through the age of 90. If his parents had not taken my advice, Penniless Perry truly would be penniless.

---

[6] 1. Penniless Perry is employed and earns $60,000 annually through age 69 (plus COLAs).
2. Penniless Perry retires at age 70 collecting Social Security Benefits of $20,000 (plus COLAs).
3. Penniless Perry at the age of 60 inherits a Roth IRA from his married widowed father, $578,548.
4. Annual living expenses, $52,000 (plus COLAs for inflation)
5. Includes a 3% Rate of Inflation and 6% Rate of Return

Are you considering navigating these potentially rocky waters without a professional who is qualified and experienced in distribution and estate planning for IRAs and retirement plans? Are you prepared to consider the interplay of the various strategic options for Social Security, Roth conversions, and retirement plan distributions? Are you clear about how marriage would affect your finances?

Please be sure to work with a trusted advisor, who can "run the numbers" for your unique situation and help you to make the ideal choices for your retirement plan, social security, Roth conversions, wills, and trusts. Avoid the pitfalls by choosing the right professional.

Final Note

I have included the level of detail and quantitative explanation in this final chapter and throughout the book because I don't offer advice like "I think you should marry your partner for financial purposes" lightly. I want you to know all the financial advantages and disadvantages of getting married before you make a decision to marry or stay single. I also want you to take the appropriate actions after you get married or if you are already married. I hope I have proven to you, that subject to limited exceptions, most same-sex couples when at least one partner is 60 or older would be significantly financially better off if they got married. You would also be better off taking some of the pro-active steps outlined in the book after you get married.

I really want you to act on what you have read. If you are in a long-term committed relationship, either on your own or preferably with the help of the appropriate advisor or advisors, make a plan and then implement the steps to achieve your plan. If you do, drop me a line. I would love to hear from you.

Valuable Resources

*Everyone needs a good financial
game plan to Retire Secure.*

— Jim Lange

About the Author

James Lange, CPA, Attorney, and registered investment advisor started the first website dedicated to estate planning for same-sex couples in Pittsburgh, **www. outestateplanning.com**, in 2002. With over 30 years of retirement and estate planning experience, he is a nationally recognized IRA, 401(k), and retirement plan distribution expert.

Lange and his team have drafted over 2,000 wills and trusts and Jim's recommendations have appeared 35 times in *The Wall Street Journal*. His articles have appeared in *Journal of Retirement Planning*, *Financial Planning*, *The Tax Adviser (AICPA)*, and *The Bottom Line*. His most recent articles have appeared in *The Pennsylvania Lawyer Magazine*, where he wrote *"The Demise of DOMA: New Financial Planning Strategies for Same-Sex Couples"* and the prestigious *Trusts and Estates* magazine in which he wrote 2 articles for same-sex and unmarried couples, *"Optimizing IRAs and Retirement Plan Distributions: Can marriage make a difference in wealth?"* and *"Optimizing Social Security Benefits for Unmarried or Same-Sex Couples: Quantifying the financial advantages of marriage."*

Jim is the author of two best-selling books, *Retire Secure! Pay Taxes Later* (Wiley 2006, 2009, 2015) and *The Roth Revolution: Pay Taxes Once and Never Again* (Morgan James 2011). Both books were endorsed by dozens of financial professionals and industry giants such as Charles Schwab, Larry King, Ed Slott, Jane Bryant Quinn, Roger Ibbotson, Burton Malkiel, Bob Keebler, and Natalie Choate. He is also the creator of the best and most flexible estate plan for IRA and retirement plan owners, **Lange's Cascading Beneficiary Plan** as well as the founder of the financial advisors educational program, **The Roth IRA Institute**.

Jim lives in Pittsburgh, in the home he grew up in, with his wife, Cindy, and their daughter, Erica. When Jim is not devising new strategies for same-sex couples, retirees, and other clients to save taxes and accumulate wealth (which is most of the time), he enjoys bicycling, hiking, skiing, and traveling with his family. Jim also plays chess and bridge both online and with his friends.

Looking For More Proven Wealth-Building Strategies from Lange Financial Group, LLC?

Check out these online resources…yours *FREE!*

The OutEstatePlanning Newsletter

The *OutEstatePlanning Newsletter* is a favorite resource for our LGBT clients and friends. In this newsletter you will get classic retirement and estate planning tools, partnered with LGBT related news and legal stories as well as updates on our Same-Sex Couple workshops and much more.

Please visit **www.outestateplanning.com** to learn more about our services and sign up for the email newsletter.

The Lange Letter

With 5,000+ subscribers, our e-mail newsletter, *The Lange Letter*, is a popular resource with our friends and clients. In this bi-weekly e-mail, you get a never ending stream of news as well as a review of classic tax-cutting and estate-building ideas.

Please visit **www.paytaxeslater.com** and sign up for your free subscription to *The Lange Letter* today and download a FREE Bonus Report which will be a valuable supplement to this book.

The Lange Money Hour Online Archive

In 2010, we started **The Lange Money Hour: Where Smart Money Talks,** a financial radio show that we think provides the best audio information on the topics of IRAs and retirement plans available anywhere. We have had some of the top financial, legal, and IRA experts as guests over the years. These luminaries include such industry greats as John Bogle (the founder of Vanguard), Jane Bryant Quinn, Ed Slott, Natalie Choate, Bob Keebler, Roger Ibbotson, Jonathan Clements, and dozens more.

We have transcribed the shows as well as added subtitles of topics covered during the shows. We are in the never ending process of attempting to help you find the information you want as quickly as possible.

With over 150 hours of solid content, these audio files and transcriptions are a great resource and are available for free at **www.paytaxeslater.com**.

Want to Learn More from Jim Lange, Attorney and CPA?

Introducing

Personal Financial Growth Products from Retire Secure Press, LLC

We are committed to helping grow your wealth.

— Jim Lange

2-Hour General Audience DVDs

- **Cut Taxes on Your IRA Withdrawals: More Money for You and for Your Heirs** – *Updated for 2015*

  My classic IRA workshop reveals the most important things you need to know about IRAs, Social Security, Roth IRA conversions, and the best estate plan for married couples. $97

- **Enhanced Social Security Planning: Getting the Most Out of Your Social Security Benefits** – *Updated for 2015*

  This DVD, partly based on a peer-reviewed Social Security article I wrote for *Trusts & Estates* magazine, "runs the numbers" on different

Social Security strategies for married couples. Getting Roth IRA conversions and Social Security right can literally make a difference of hundreds of thousands of dollars. $97

- **What Every IRA Owner Should Know About Roth IRAs and Roth IRA Conversions** – *Updated for 2015*

  This is my classic Roth IRA workshop. If you have an IRA or retirement plan, you and your family could benefit significantly by using the techniques in this DVD. In fact, I used to charge $10,000 to present this same information to financial advisors. $97

- **Who Says You Can't Control from the Grave? The Appropriate Use of Trusts to Protect Your Family** – *Updated for 2015*

  Get the full picture on the appropriate use of trusts. This DVD covers how and when to avoid probate, plus trusts for minors, spendthrifts, and beneficiaries with special needs. Also discussed is the increasingly popular, "I don't want my no-good son/daughter-in-law to inherit one red cent trust." $97

Special: Want the Best Deal of All? *(Shown on page 125)*

Get all **4 updated DVDs for $197** and as our way of thanking you, we will include the following 3 CDs as bonuses:

1. **The Best of The Lange Money Hour: Where Smart Money Talks**

   This is a compilation of some of the highlights of 130 radio shows. Guests: John Bogle, Jane Bryant Quinn, Ed Slott, Robert Cass, P.J. DiNuzzo, Joe Hurley, Paul Merriman, Grant Oliphant, Natalie Choate, and Roger Ibbotson (CD 60 minutes)

2. **Using Nobel Prize Research to Maximize Your Investment Return**

   Guest: Paul Merriman, author, journalist, and nationally recognized expert on index funds, asset allocation, and financial management strategies. (CD 50 minutes)

3. **Following an Efficient Strategy Produces Dividends**

   Guest: P.J. DiNuzzo, a nationally recognized expert in investment management and our partner in passive index investment management. P.J. and his firm rank in the top 1% of America's more than 800,000 investment advisors. (CD 50 minutes)

Please go to **www.jameslange.com** for product details and order forms.

2-Hour Niche Market DVDs

For Professors and University Faculty:

- **Cut Taxes on Your TIAA-CREF, Vanguard and IRA Withdrawals: More Money for University Faculty and Their Heirs**

  This DVD covers the most important financial issues for current and retired faculty members. Get unique recommendations for one of life's great mysteries: "How do I get money out of TIAA when I retire?" It also provides strategies that are in your best interest, not your financial advisor's best interest. $97.

For Same-Sex Couples:

- **Live Gay, Retire Rich: New Financial Planning Strategies for Same-Sex Couples**

  Same-sex couples have great opportunities to provide for the financially weaker partner by getting married. This DVD guides you and your partner through the complexities of taking advantage of the financial prospects now available. In particular, the issues of inheriting IRAs and collecting spousal benefits for Social Security are examined in detail. $97

- **New Estate Planning Strategies for Same-Sex Couples with IRA and Retirement Plans**

  New thinking about estate planning after a series of changes in federal and state laws is essential to protect and provide for yourself and your partner. Learn what you need to know in this highly specialized DVD. $97

Books

- *Retire Secure!: A Guide to Getting the Most out of What You've Got* ($24.95)

  Now more than ever, Americans approaching or already in retirement are asking, "Will my money last as long as I do and what can I do to make sure I get the most from what I've got?" In this updated Third Edition of *Retire*

Secure!, Jim provides new examples and strategies developed from his 32 years as a practicing estate attorney and CPA.

The third edition shows how to use IRAs, retirement plans, Roth IRAs and Roth 401(k)s, Roth IRA conversions, as well as other tax-favored strategies to let Uncle Sam subsidize your retirement and your family's lifestyle for the remainder of your life, your spouse's life, and long beyond that.

Jim has a history of seeing ahead of the curve and in this edition, he analyzes the possible repercussions if Congress kills the "Stretch IRA" or seriously truncates its stretch. But, he also provides new avenues to reach the best outcomes if the laws are changed. For example he shows how using a Charitable Remainder Unitrust (CRUT) as a beneficiary of your IRA will potentially be more favorable for many families than just leaving an IRA to your children.

Every chapter of *Retire Secure!* contains recommendations, analysis, and case studies based on a deep understanding of tax law, estate planning, investing, and running the numbers. Most importantly, they are time tested and proven to work.

- *The Roth Revolution: Pay Taxes Once and Never Again* ($19.44)

In essence, a Roth IRA conversion requires paying taxes on the portion of your IRA or 401(k) that you convert, but then that money can grow income tax-free for the rest of your, your spouse's, your children's and grandchildren's lives. The advantage of a tax-savvy long-term Roth IRA conversion is often measured in the millions. The real eye-opener, however, is that Roth IRA conversions are great for older IRA owners, regardless of the benefits to future generations.

The Roth Revolution addresses the following topics clearly and objectively:

1. Whether, how much, and when to convert

2. Costs and benefits of a Roth IRA conversion

3. Advice for taxpayers in each income tax bracket

4. The impact of future tax increases

5. Synergy of delaying (or returning) Social Security and Roth IRA conversions

6. Combining charitable gifts and Roth IRA conversions

7. Tax-free conversions of after-tax dollars in IRAs and retirement plans

8. Converting and recharacterizing strategies

You may be asking, "Who in their right mind would pay taxes before they have to?" The answer is James Lange and thousands of his readers and clients, all the top IRA experts, and after reading *The Roth Revolution*, hopefully you will too.

- *Live Gay, Retire Rich!* ($19.95)

There were two gay couples with identical financial resources. They each had the same amount of money, identical investments, identical taxes, and identical earnings history for Social Security purposes.

The first couple did no planning. The second gay couple followed the advice offered in *Live Gay, Retire Rich!* Doing reasonable projections, the first couple runs out of money in 28 years while the second couple has $1.4 million dollars and their portfolio continues to increase.

What was the difference? The first couple never got married, started Social Security at 62, didn't make any Roth IRA conversions, and didn't use key IRA, retirement plan and estate planning strategies. The second gay couple did get married, used our recommended apply and suspend technique for Social Security, did a series of Roth IRA conversions, and used key IRA, retirement plan and estate planning strategies.

Live Gay, Retire Rich! gives same-sex couples the knowledge they need to get their retirement right!

Please go to **www.jameslange.com** for product details and order forms.

Free Informational DVDs and Audio CDs

- **Index vs. Active Investing: Nobel Prize Winning Research Sheds Light on Investing**

  Learn the distinctions between the two philosophies of investing and also why we are huge fans of Dimensional Fund Advisors (DVD 30 minutes)

- **How We Sabotage our Retirement Planning and Why Index Investing Offers the Best Solution**

This is the longer version of our investing DVD with more background and details on the advantages of index investing. (DVD 110 minutes)

For more videos, recommended reading lists, and an audio archive of all of our radio shows be sure to visit **www.jameslange.com**.

Here is a detailed overview of just one of Jim's classic workshops captured on DVD for IRA owners:

- **Cut Taxes on Your IRA Withdrawals: More Money for You and for Your Heirs**

Many people underestimate the value of coordinating multiple strategies that, in concert, form a cohesive financial plan designed to yield the best results over time.

Among those decisions which require coordination are: timing your IRA distributions, your Roth IRA strategy, and your Social Security distributions. Comprehensive planning, when done properly, can preserve your IRAs, retirement plan, and Roth IRAs long after you are gone.

James Lange has devoted a lot of energy to educating financial advisors and consumers about the strategies he has been using with his clients for decades. He founded **The Roth IRA Institute**™ to provide financial professionals with the tools they need to educate their clients. For consumers, his two-hour workshop titled *Cut Taxes on Your IRA Withdrawals: More Money for You and Your Heirs* has been drawing record crowds for years.

Now, Jim wants to get this important information into the hands of all taxpayers. He realizes that people across the country are searching for these answers but are unable to travel to one of his workshops. They may want to see and hear, rather than just read about these strategies in *Retire Secure!* With that in mind, Jim is making his current live workshops available to everyone in a package that contains a DVD plus transcript. With this DVD of the live workshop, you can learn from participant's questions and Jim's answers.

Now You Can Experience Jim Lange's Workshops from the Comfort of Your Own Home!

Even if you've already read Jim's books—you'll gain valuable insights from Jim's *Cut Taxes on Your IRA Withdrawals* workshop. This workshop covers optimal distribution planning for IRA and retirement plan owners, Roth IRA conversions, and tax-savvy methods of preserving IRA and Roth IRA to pass to your heirs. It is geared toward investors between the ages of 60 and 75 with $250,000 or more in their retirement plans, but the information is of benefit to people of all ages and financial situations. Here's what you'll discover:

- The tax-savvy way to spend different classes of assets in retirement.
- The "secret" of the Roth IRA and why it's such a powerful retirement planning tool.
- How you can enjoy tax-free growth with a Roth IRA conversion.
- Coordinating the timing between Roth IRA conversions and Social Security distributions.
- A little-known technique for making a Roth IRA conversion while legally avoiding certain taxes.
- Accumulation strategies if you're still working.
- Peer-reviewed articles discussing the benefits of a Roth IRA conversion.
- And much, much more!

We invite you to visit our website **www.jameslange.com** for a full list of resources including books, DVDs, CDs, and easy access to our radio show—**The Lange Money Hour**—archives. Some products are for sale, but many are free or available for streaming.

Visit www.jameslange.com for more details.

Applying the Strategies in this Book to Your Personal Situation to Help You Get the Most out of What You've Got

Working With the Lange Financial Group

Okay. Let's say you want to follow the proven strategies for retirement investing presented in this book. *We can help.*

Our team of CPAs, estate attorneys and money managers apply the concepts of this book to help our client's cut taxes and retire securely. Then, we help them strategically pass on whatever is left.

Lange Financial Group, LLC has been working with same-sex couples and Pittsburgh's LGBT community for over a decade. Back in 2002, we started the first website in Pittsburgh dedicated to estate planning for gay couples. We individualize all of our clients planning, but LGBT clients frequently require planning that falls outside of conventional planning protocols. With the rapid change of laws over the last few years, same-sex couples are afforded many more rights than in the past, but they still have unique opportunities that call upon the complex problem solving abilities of our entire professional group.

The CPA firm, the law firm, and the investment advisory firm are all owned by me, Jim Lange, and operate under the same roof in Pittsburgh, PA. Clients benefit by having skilled professionals in different disciplines working together to develop an integrated and comprehensive long-term plan—always with the client's best interest in mind. Preparing wills, trusts, and related legal work is handled through the law firm and is only available for Pennsylvania residents. Our Investment Advisory services are handled separately, and are available to clients in Pennsylvania, New York, Ohio, Virginia, Florida, and California.

Our team of CPAs "run the numbers" to help determine the best strategies for our clients' IRAs and retirement plans, and develop a tax-savvy estate plan. They also run the numbers for strategies not covered in *Live Gay, Retire*

Rich! such as developing an optimal Roth IRA conversion plan that might include annual Roth IRA conversions over a certain number of years. Beyond running the numbers, we provide something else: a big-picture perspective. For instance, we may discover that a client who assumed he has to work an additional five years actually has sufficient income to retire tomorrow. Or, he can continue to work, but on his own terms. Observations like these can be life-changing—and liberating.

We also address other pressing retirement concerns, such as, how much money can you afford to spend and never run out of money? or would it be possible to spend winters in Florida, and summers at home? Information gathered from "running the numbers" and an big-picture perspective, could help take the guesswork out of making difficult decisions.

Because managing money is more than a full-time job (as is keeping up with the "ins and outs" of the legal and tax system), we do not manage investments internally at Lange Financial Group, LLC. Instead, we looked at the universe of possibilities and determined what the best options would be for our clients.

Happily, we found two first-class organizations right in our backyard. DiNuzzo Index Advisors, who offers what we believe are the best low-cost index funds on the planet, has become our main go-to resource for our clients who are looking for professionally managed portfolios. For clients who prefer an active money management style, we collaborate with Fort Pitt Capital Group.

When you and your partner or spouse become clients of the Lange Financial Group, LLC, you will benefit from the integrated experience of our financial professionals—all of whom have different but complementary expertise. In essence, you are getting what we think are the best retirement and estate planning strategies for the often complex planning issues of same-sex couples, along with the best money management services that I know of. For our combined services, you pay a fee that will fall between one-half of one percent and one percent of the money we actually manage (the fee depends on how much money is invested).

Your Single Source for Planning, Tax and Investment Advice

So what do you stand to gain from our coordinated strategy? Frequently, individuals will have a lawyer, an investment advisor, a CPA, and maybe even an insurance broker. But communication among those professionals is frequently nonexistent. The result is a collection of professionals presumably all working with the client's best interest at heart, but without a comprehensive strategy. Unfortunately, an absence or a lack of communication among these professionals can lead to serious mistakes.

With our "one-stop-shop" approach, you can benefit from the best integrated strategies for your IRA and retirement plans, Social Security strategy, investments, as well as wills, trusts, and estate planning needs.

There are relatively new (and valuable) opportunities for most LGBT families, particularly with respect to Social Security, IRAs, and retirement plans. We believe that having experts in different fields all under the same roof is the most effective model for integrated retirement and estate planning. We do offer clients a choice of money managers, but these days, we advise most of our new clients to have their money managed using the best low-cost index advisory firm we know, DiNuzzo Index Advisors, Inc. DiNuzzo Index Advisors, Inc. invests money through Dimensional Fund Advisors or "DFA" who we believe manage the best set of low-cost index funds on the planet.

We think this multidiscipline approach is a win/win/win.

It is a win for us because we get to do what we do best: implement our tax and estate planning strategies and help people retire securely and wisely pass on what's available to their heirs. With the client's permission (which they always provide), we share our recommendations with DiNuzzo Index Advisors, Inc.

It is a win for DiNuzzo Index Advisors, Inc. because they get to do what they do best: manage money, but always taking the big picture into account.

The biggest winner, however, is the client.

- **You get our practical advice—including the financial ramifications of getting married. You get our statistical advice that comes as a result of our running the numbers.**

- **You get comprehensive retirement and estate planning, and integrated money management using low-cost index funds - all for one low fee of between 50 basis points and 1%.**

Our association with DiNuzzo Index Advisors, Inc., is growing at roughly $60 million per year of assets-under-management. We are expecting to grow even faster in the future. At press time, we have roughly $180 million under

management with DiNuzzo Index Advisors, Inc. We enjoy a 99% client retention rate with our mutual Lange/DiNuzzo clients.

What follows is a firm history. If that doesn't interest you, please skip to
the next section, **Lange Financial Group Today**.

How Lange Financial Group Got Started

Frankly, it was *only recently* that I pinpointed what I wanted to be when I grew
up. That might sound funny coming from a middle-aged man and a long-time
business professional, but I find that re-thinking my mission in life, from time
to time, keeps important distinctions fresh and top-of-mind. So here goes: I
want to be the best, most trusted financial advisor in the area, leading the best
team of CPAs, estate attorneys, and money managers you can find anywhere.
And I want as many people in as many walks of life as possible, to benefit from
the expertise my firm offers.

But my aspirations didn't start out that high.

When I started out after college in 1978, I worked at a small CPA firm
and did some moonlighting preparing tax returns. As my side business grew,
I opened my first office in my mother's house. Many of my long-time clients
remember that walk up to the third floor.

I changed my "day job" to working in the Tax Department of Arthur Ander-
sen (formerly a big 8 CPA firm) and later Buchanan Ingersoll (a big Pittsburgh
corporate law firm) and continued to grow my side business while I attended
Duquesne University School of Law at night. It was a busy time. When I finished law school in 1984, I gave up corporate America and hung out shingles
for both a CPA firm and a law firm. My practice concentrated exclusively on
taxes, wills, trusts and estates.

I started (and continue) to work with clients who were "IRA heavy," mean-
ing they had more money in their IRAs and retirement plans than outside their
IRAs and retirement plans. How did they get that way? Generally speaking, the
IRA and retirement plan owners I work with today are and were prudent savers.

While they were working, it was hard to save money because of bills, taxes,
groceries, a mortgage, the car payments, the children's braces, college tuition
costs, etc. But, despite the expenses, they didn't take their future for granted.
They generally contributed money into their retirement plans at work, and
took advantage of employer matching programs if they were available.

Upon retirement, they often have between $500,000 and $3 million in their retirement plans, two modestly priced cars, a house that is paid for, kids who are finally out of the house, and not much else. So, to best serve their needs, I knew I had to become an IRA and retirement plan strategy expert.

As part of my journey, I studied IRA literature extensively, especially "the bible" on IRAs and retirement plans, *Life and Death Planning for Retirement Benefits*, by Natalie Choate, Esq. This is a 500+ page book basically written in IRS code, but full of gems.

What Natalie doesn't do, however, is run the numbers to quantify and compare the results of the different IRA and estate planning strategies she presents in her book. So I ran the numbers, and I was thrilled when I realized how many cool strategies IRA owners could take advantage of. A client's financial outcome can be dramatically different depending on the strategy he or she uses.

> **Someone who uses the best strategies, as determined by *running the numbers*, generally has much better results than the individual who *wings it*. And the individual who wings it usually never realizes they missed the best strategies because no analysis was done to figure out what the best strategies were for his or her personal situation!**
>
> **Same-sex couples run an even higher risk of missing out, as they have not before had the legal right to take advantage of some of these strategies.**

"Let's run the numbers" became our mantra. Then and now **we offer our assets under management clients immediate and long-term advice backed up with solid quantitative analysis and excellent statistics**—this, in particular, appeals to our discerning clientele.

Over the years, I put together a crackerjack team of estate attorneys and CPAs, including several "number crunchers" extraordinaire. Together we expanded the scope of running the numbers to include testing different levels of spending in retirement, maximizing Roth IRA conversions, optimizing Social Security benefits, and analyzing different methods and amounts of gifting including 529 plans for grandchildren's education, sophisticated estate planning strategies, and other relevant issues.

Add Roth IRA Conversions into the Mix

In 1997, a whole new type of retirement plan called a Roth IRA was proposed by Congress. I knew this was going to be a great thing for most IRA and retirement plan owners, but especially for my IRA heavy clients. Even before the law took effect, I ran more numbers that specifically tested the advantages of Roth IRAs and Roth IRA conversions.

Again, I was astounded by the results. **I knew that making the appropriate Roth IRA conversion recommendations for the right people at the right time could mean hundreds of thousands of dollars in reduced taxes and additional tax-free wealth for them.** And when I continued the analysis to the next generation, I saw that taking my advice could mean millions of additional dollars for their children and grandchildren. I also began to see the huge advantages that marriage provides in passing along generational wealth, and the inherent disadvantages to couples who couldn't marry, even if they wished to. It was around this time that I began to think about strategies we could use to help LGBT couples gain a more equal financial footing.

I wrote the first peer-reviewed article on Roth IRAs and Roth IRA conversions for the American Institute of CPAs Tax Division journal, *The Tax Adviser*. That article catapulted me into national standing as a Roth IRA expert, author and speaker. But more importantly, my clients benefitted when we began to apply the principles of my tested and peer-reviewed Roth IRA and Roth IRA conversion analysis and "ran the numbers" for their individual situations.

Articles, Radio Shows and Books

I continued writing articles for many financial journals including *The Journal of Retirement Planning*, *The Tax Adviser*, and *Bottom Line* and many more. As recently as 2014, we published two peer-reviewed articles in *Trusts & Estates* magazine: *"Optimizing IRAs and Retirement Plan Distributions, Can Marriage Make a Difference in Wealth"* and *"Optimizing Social Security Benefits for Unmarried or Same-Sex Couples, Quantifying the Financial Advantages of Marriage."* Our strategies have been featured in *The Wall Street Journal* 35 times.

In 2010, we started **The Lange Money Hour: Where Smart Money Talks**; a financial radio show that we think provides the best audio information on IRAs and retirement plans available anywhere. We have produced over 150 shows, many with the top financial, legal, and IRA experts as guests—industry giants such as John Bogle (the founder of Vanguard), Jane Bryant Quinn, Jonathan Clements, Ed Slott, Natalie Choate, Bob Keebler, Roger Ibbotson (all on multiple times), and dozens more. Our guests have written some of the top financial books of our time. In preparation for the shows, I read most of the books and prepare the questions. Having this much access to the top financial minds of our time is thrilling and has been a true education for me and my listeners.

But I also wanted to write an encompassing retirement and estate planning book with solid recommendations backed by concrete proof. Furthermore, I wanted to provide a detailed explanation of how you could enjoy a much better lifestyle by making the best strategic decisions for your IRAs and retirement and estate plans. I wrote *Retire Secure!* (Wiley 2006 & 2009), and I was pleased to get glowing reviews from some of the top people in the field, including Charles Schwab, Jane Bryant Quinn, Larry King, Ed Slott, Roger Ibbotson and virtually all the nationally known IRA experts. I just finished the third edition.

Although I discussed Roth IRAs and Roth IRA conversion analysis in all three editions of *Retire Secure!*, I also knew the entire Roth IRA conversion subject required a dedicated book , so I wrote and published *The Roth Revolution, Pay Taxes Once and Never Again* (Morgan James, 2010) to fill the gap. This book, *Live Gay, Retire Rich!*, is the second edition of a book I adapted from *Retire Secure!*, and specifically addresses the retirement and estate planning problems of same-sex couples.

The publication of these books led to prestigious speaking engagements around the country, and I was hired to educate financial professionals throughout the United States. Interestingly, it became very clear to me, after speaking to and with thousands of financial advisors, that very few retirees were receiving great proactive retirement and estate planning advice *combined* with good investment advice.

History of Collaborating with Money Managers

Since I wanted to do the work described above but not handle the actual money management component, I knew I had to collaborate with the top money management firms I could find. My first collaboration was with Fort Pitt Capital Group, Inc., an excellent money management firm using an active management approach (see below for details). Then, I started working with DiNuzzo Index Advisors, Inc.

The History of Working with DiNuzzo Index Advisors, Inc.

A significant turning point for my company was when I learned about low-cost index investing and what I believe to be the best set of index funds on the planet, Dimensional Funds (offered through Dimensional Fund Advisors, also known as DFA). After learning of their great philosophy and strong performance results, I wanted to represent DFA myself.

But DFA is very fussy about the advisors they will allow to represent their funds, and my application was rejected. They declined to approve me because they knew of my collaboration with Fort Pitt Capital Group, Inc., an excellent active money management firm that we also work with (described below). DFA told me they only appoint advisors who work exclusively with index funds.

I explained that I wanted to give my clients a choice between active money management and low-cost index money management, or possibly a combination of the two. They maintained that the only way I could become a DFA provider was by dropping my association with Fort Pitt Capital Group, Inc., which I was not willing to do. Accordingly, DFA and I went our separate ways.

Years later, I was talking with a colleague from California, and he told me how happy his clients were with DFA. He had a hard time believing that they had rejected me as, by this time, I was a fairly well-known IRA expert with three best-selling books. He recommended I contact a friend of his who works for DFA. His friend asked me to send him my books and he would at least consider making an exception to their rule. As it turned out, the DFA contact liked my books enough to approve my firm as a DFA provider.

That was great, but I still faced a dilemma. I am not really qualified—nor do I have the time to become qualified—to provide expert money management services. Then I had another idea. I asked Dimensional Fund Advisors and other industry experts who they believed was the best DFA provider in western Pennsylvania. And that is how I met P. J. DiNuzzo.

I contacted P. J. DiNuzzo, and we came to an arrangement. He and his firm, DiNuzzo Index Advisors, Inc. would handle the money management responsibilities for our clients, and our firm would continue to "run the numbers" and provide advice on Roth IRA conversions, estate planning, Social Security planning, safe withdrawal rates, and other financial strategies. The arrangement is quite similar to the one I have with Fort Pitt Capital Group, Inc. Having these associations with Fort Pitt Capital Group, Inc. and DiNuzzo Index Advisors, Inc. leaves me open to focus on what I and my team love—financial calculations and strategizing—rather than money management.

I have similar arrangements (described above) with several other money management firms, however, the two most significant firms, and the ones I will discuss in this book, are Fort Pitt Capital Group, Inc. and DiNuzzo Index Advisors, Inc.

Lange Financial Group Today

Fort Pitt Capital Group, Inc.

For more than a decade, I've had a working relationship with Fort Pitt Capital Group, Inc., an independent Registered Investment Advisor (RIA) with an impressive track record. Clients who are interested in "active" investment management (as opposed to an index approach) are referred to them for portfolio management. Clients pay an annual management fee of 1% or less, depending on how much is invested. For this fee, clients get the benefit of our tax planning strategies and other financial advice listed above, as well as Fort Pitt Capital Group, Inc.'s money management expertise and services. This collaboration continues to work very well.

Fort Pitt Capital Group, Inc. has their own processes that they go through before they accept an individual as a client. For example, they produce a written investment plan for all prospective clients. Services for ongoing clients include quarterly performance reporting, periodic investment plan updates and regular meetings to discuss life events or changes that might affect portfolio goals or risk tolerance. The bottom line—our firms combine to provide a powerful blend of planning and money management that we believe is unequaled in the Pittsburgh marketplace for active money management.

DiNuzzo Index Advisors, Inc.

P. J. DiNuzzo and his firm, DiNuzzo Index Advisors, Inc. (DIA) use Dimensional Fund Advisor funds, which I believe are the best set of low-cost index funds on the planet. P. J. DiNuzzo has put together a superb team of CFPs, ChFCs, CPAs, MBAs and financial advisors, and they have been serving their clients brilliantly since 1989. P. J. and his team are truly the hardest working group of financial advisors I know.

DIA conducts an extensive financial analysis, including constructing a personal balance sheet and a personal income statement. They focus on investment decisions, asset allocation, and diversification.

Their process is in-depth and impressively client focused. It includes two to three meetings before they even agree to manage a client's money. One of the strategies P.J. and his team use to benefit our mutual clients is the DiNuzzo Money Bucket Stack Analysis™ (DMBSA). With this strategy, P.J. separates the client's investible assets into different accounts or "buckets" based on the time periods and purposes in which the client anticipates using those assets.

Each client may have an account or "bucket" for current expenses, and for money needed within the next two years for necessities. This "bucket" of money is invested conservatively, so that clients have the peace of mind in knowing that fluctuations in the market will not affect their immediate needs. They may also have a "legacy bucket" with money that they never intend to touch in their lifetimes; this bucket may be invested with a longer horizon. We would likely fund the "legacy bucket" with Roth IRAs, another way our tax strategies and their investment planning combine in an effort to produce the best results for our clients.

Many clients have four or five different "money buckets" with various allocations, allowing them to enjoy a higher level of comfort in the market and to avoid unnecessary risks with funds they are counting on for support and retirement. The ultimate goal: to combine our strategies and to optimize the client's potential return within a risk category that suits their preferences and volatility/loss tolerance.

Then, after both P.J. and his team develop an investment plan, and we develop a comprehensive retirement and estate plan, we help our mutual client implement the plan. But our involvement doesn't end there.

All good plans need to be modified and adjusted due to changing circumstances—portfolios increase and decrease because of market conditions, children marry, grandchildren are born, and divorces happen. That's why clients meet with someone from our firm at least once on an annual basis to update their numbers, and with P.J.'s team on a semi-annual or annual basis to review portfolio performance. The DiNuzzo team also manages a client's portfolio using a "best practice" in the industry called "regular rebalancing."

Suffice it to say, the arrangement has been a win-win-win. **Our clients see the value in our combined services. And as I said, we have 99% retention rate for all the clients we share.** It has been an interesting and rewarding journey, but I am far from complacent.

I firmly believe that a lot of that success and client retention has to do with our team. I have an extremely loyal team of accomplished professionals who all chip in to bring our clients the best service possible. They include:

Glenn Venturino, CPA	27 years
Sandy Proto, Office Manager	23 years
Steve Kohman, CPA, CSEP, CSRP	19 years
Donna Master, Bookkeeper	16 years
Daryl Ross, Legal Assistant	15 years
Diane Markel, CPA	15 years
Alice Davis, Client Service Coordinator	12 years
Matt Schwartz, Attorney	12 years
Karen Mathias, Attorney	6 years
Curt Borowski, Office Assistant	5 years
Carol Palmer, Writer; Tax Preparer	4 years
Amanda Cassady-Schweinsberg, Marketing Director	3 years
Eric Emerson, Internet Marketing Director	1 year
Shirl Trefelner, CPA	1 year
Tanya Chiu, Administrative Assistant	4 mos.

With this outstanding team and the expertise of Fort Pitt Capital Group, Inc. and DiNuzzo Index Advisors, Inc., we have a formidable knowledge base to offer our clients.

Helping People with the Best Strategies

I love helping people live happier lives by helping them cut taxes, save money, and plan for retirement. Of course having more money doesn't necessarily mean you will be happy, but it sure helps. Many times, the feeling of financial security and the absence of worry about money is as important as the money we save clients.

There are all kinds of money saving strategies that professionals who *quantitatively as well as qualitatively* understand IRAs and retirement plans can recommend and implement. In fact, we have helped all of our clients, including same-sex couples, for years. By implementing many of the plans mentioned in this book, we have saved our clients tens of thousands of dollars, and sometimes even hundreds of thousands of dollars. If you consider the benefit that our planning has on future generations, some of those savings can be counted in millions of dollars.

We have also developed what we think is the best estate plan on the planet initially meant for traditionally married couples, but now available to all married couples—**Lange's Cascading Beneficiary Plan**—which is described in detail in *Retire Secure!* We incorporated that planning in the early nineties before anyone even heard of it. That plan was first published in a peer-reviewed journal in 1998 and has since been featured in *The Wall Street Journal* twice, *Newsweek*, and literally hundreds of other publications.

Over the years, we have drafted thousands of wills that include some variation of **Lange's Cascading Beneficiary Plan**. Unfortunately, as with any estate practice, some of our clients have died. Fortunately, however, our estate plans have performed exactly as we envisioned, providing enormous benefits to the survivors.

So there it is. After many years of trying to figure out what was best for my clients, I inadvertently found out what was best for me and who I truly wanted to be: A trusted advisor who, with my team, supplies the best tax-saving, Roth IRA conversion, Social Security, retirement and estate planning advice that you can find.

The Client Experience: What You Can Expect When You Work With Lange Financial Group, LLC

Running the Numbers

Once a client signs up for the combined services of Lange Financial Group, LLC and one of our investment advisors, they are entitled to multiple "running the numbers" sessions with Lange Financial Group, LLC.

The first session usually concentrates on determining the best tax and financial strategies for the client; when and how much of a Roth IRA conversion would be advisable; how much money can safely be spent in retirement; determining if gifts are appropriate and, if so, what type of gifts, and how much and when.

Frequently, the client asks questions like: "Does it make financial sense for my partner and I to marry?" "Can we afford a second house and if so, how much house can we afford?"; "Should I take a lump sum or a monthly pension?"; "If I take a pension, what terms should I choose?"; and "What is the best way to address my grandchildren's education?" These "running the numbers" consultation services are provided by my team at Lange Financial Group, LLC.

Our veteran "number runner" is Steve Kohman, a CPA with 30+ years of experience. Steve did the original "number running" for the first two editions of *Retire Secure!,* and has also done the projection analysis for many of our publications and many of our assets-under-management clients. We also have on board Shirl Trefelner, CPA, who did much of the updated analysis for the third edition and also runs the numbers for our clients.

We also run the numbers so that we can calculate how to maximize a client's Social Security benefits (not covered in this book, but something we do in our practice). Karen Mathias, one of our estate attorneys/tax preparers made an extensive study of Social Security strategies, and we have learned to use excellent Social Security optimization software. Obviously, we do the analysis based on the client's individual situation including their earnings record, current age and health, and both current and former marital status.

Sometimes the financial issues that we address can be resolved in one meeting, though more commonly we schedule two meetings to make sure that all of the client's concerns are satisfied. We have run numbers for hundreds of clients, including many engineers, scientists, CPAs, and many others. I was even hired to run the numbers for two of my former bosses! These sessions often lead to proactive strategies that significantly improve the financial future of our clients and their descendants.

We prefer to have the client in the room while we are doing our calculations. That way, clients see where we are getting our numbers from, and we can explain why we are making the recommendations that we make. It isn't simply a matter of sticking numbers into a spread sheet; there is a great deal of critical thinking that goes into picking the right numbers and hypothesizing realistic scenarios.

Furthermore, clients can pose their own "what if" scenarios on the spot. Our team members have the skill to adapt the numbers for virtually any scenario. If you have a particular concern, we can address it. As with all projections, we have to make some assumptions, but no one can predict with certainty what will happen in the future. Projections that include reasonable assumptions, or even a range of projections with different assumptions, can help determine the best strategies possible.

Another unique feature of the way we run the numbers is that we use multiple professional software programs to arrive at our conclusions, including our customized in-house adaption of an Excel spreadsheet. At this point, there is no one software program that allows users to enter a lot of data, hit the "optimize" button, and have it provide the definitive answer.

The skill and experience of the "number runner" is far more important than the choice of software that we employ. When we think we have the best strategy, we test it – not only with the "number running" software, but also with sophisticated tax preparation software.

We input the data from a client's entire tax return, plus our proposed solution just to make sure there are no surprises. Sometimes we are surprised. For example, sometimes we encounter an unexpected tax increase or decrease that may be a consequence of the alternative minimum tax, the phase-out of itemized deductions, taxes on Social Security and/or Medicare Part B, etc.

When this happens, we adjust our recommendations. **The beauty of running the numbers and testing them before we implement anything is that adjustments that need to be made are done well in advance. That way we catch the issues, not the IRS.**

Finally, when we arrive at what we and the client thinks is the best long-term strategy, we work with DiNuzzo Index Advisors, Inc. or Fort Pitt Capital Group, Inc. (depending on which management style the client is most comfortable with); we also help implement the investment part of that strategy.

Experience and Perspective

Another dimension our firm adds is experience and perspective. We often get involved in areas where the "solution" is obvious to us without running the numbers. Here are some examples where our experience and perspective has made a difference to clients and the way they live their lives.

We've told people:

- Getting married is going to save you hundreds of thousands of dollars in estate taxes, and allow you to collect thousands of extra dollars in Social Security benefits.

- You have enough money to retire and the decision to work or retire should be based on what you want to do, not on money. (One professor client commented, "I am not going to quit tomorrow, but I am not going to take any **** from the chair anymore.

- You have enough money to become "snowbirds," and you can enjoy that lifestyle without running out of money.

- You need to think about pre-and post-nuptial agreements to protect your children (a difficult subject at the best of times and an outsider's perspective can be a great help). Or, if you rejected the idea because you didn't want to start a fight, you might want to think about the "I don't want my no good son-in-law to inherit one red cent of my money trust."

- You might want to think about the timing and the best types of gifts for your children and grandchildren.

- You want to move to a state that has a higher tax rate? With your $5 million, you can. You should live where you want to live, even if taxes are higher.

In Conclusion

Business models change over time (as mine has), and I imagine there will be additional changes ahead. I feel like I am well on my way to achieving my dream of being the best, most inclusive, and most trusted advisor I can be. I have done this by always putting my client's interests above my own.

Many of the strategies I advocate (maxing out retirement plans, doing Roth IRA conversions, waiting for as long as possible to collect Social Security, using existing assets and retirement plans if appropriate) actually reduce my compensation. But, ultimately that doesn't matter. I want to be on the same side as my clients, not have competing interests!

After all, isn't that what we all want from our service providers? Are the plumbers and mechanics of the world acting in their clients' best interests? I hope so. Would they offer the same advice and charge the same fee to trusting consumers as they would to savvy retired plumbers or mechanics? That's what I do—I give the same quality honest advice to all my clients, no matter who they are.

I run my business the way that I do because I believe that advisors who act with their clients' best interests at heart feel better about what they are doing.

Call it karma if you like but, in the long run, trusted advisors acting in their clients' best interests lead happier lives.

When you care and do the right thing for the client it shows. I walk around my community with confidence knowing that I can look everyone I meet in the eye with no fear of being seen as "that lousy advisor who took advantage of me." I have known many of my clients for decades. I have been with them through marriages and divorces, triumphs and tragedies, births and deaths. Being their trusted advisor gives me a profound sense of satisfaction and purpose. We are growing old together, and I really like that.

Thank you for investing the time to read my book. I hope it helps you on the way to becoming who and where you want to be—personally and financially.

Are You Interested in Working with Lange Financial Group, LLC?

To find out if the combination of our services and our "one-stop-shop" business model works for you, I am offering a limited number of FREE initial consultations for those who qualify.* During every initial consultation, we will go over your current estate planning documents, your tax returns, your investments, and discuss your primary goals.

If it seems like we can have a mutually compatible relationship, then we analyze your portfolio using an objective reporting service. As a part of this initial consultation we also prepare extensive recommendations designed to help you achieve your ideal retirement and estate plan, and we will supplement our recommendations by providing you with all the books, CDs, DVDs that we think are relevant for your situation (we will even prioritize the most important ones to read, listen to, or watch).

If you like our initial recommendations, then you will meet with the appropriate members of our teams to further refine your plan (i.e., our legal or tax team; or P. J. DiNuzzo and his investment team; or a Fort Pitt Capital Group, Inc. representative).

If all the relationships seem compatible, and you feel that the planning is right for you, then we will do the paperwork and you will officially become a client (although you may already feel like one by then)! It can be a lengthy process to become a client, as we aren't the right fit for everyone, and we want to make sure you will enjoy working with us, but the results and relationships are truly worth it. We believe the thorough process is one of the reasons we enjoy a 99% retention rate with the mutual Lange/DiNuzzo clients.

To inquire about a *Free Second Opinion** please:

Call 1-800-387-1129

or go to www.retirementpittsburgh.com/bookoffer

* FREE Second Opinion meetings are reserved for those with
at least $500,000 of investible assets.

CPSIA information can be obtained at www.ICGtesting.com
Printed in the USA
LVOW10s0418230915

455356LV00002B/2/P